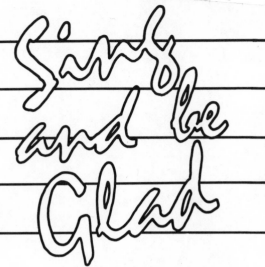

FOUNDATION SERIES
SONGS FROM GRADES 1-8

Evangel Press, Nappanee, IN 46550
Faith and Life Press, Newton, KS 67114
Mennonite Publishing House, Scottdale, PA 15683

For no other foundation can any one lay than that which is laid, which is Jesus Christ.
1 Corinthians 3:11

SING AND BE GLAD:
FOUNDATION SERIES SONGS FROM GRADES 1-8

Helen Johns, compiling editor
Laurence Martin, managing editor, The Foundation Series curriculum
Jim Caskey, cover design
Published by: the Mennonite Church, the General Conference Mennonite Church, and
the Brethren in Christ
Cooperative users: Church of the Brethren

Grateful acknowledgement is made to individuals and publishers who have granted permission for the use of their copyrighted songs in this book. The compiler has attempted to ascertain the copyright status of every selection included. If there are instances where proper credit is not given, the publishers will gladly make necessary corrections in subsequent printings.

ISBN 0-916035-13-1

Introduction

Music is fun. Music is educational. *Sing and be Glad* is designed to move the use of music closer to the heart of Christian education in your church and home, and to bring about joy and learning through singing. Chosen as likeable and singable during the years of The Foundation Series use and revision, these songs—some old, some new—deal with a wide range of Christian theology and experience. Of course, we couldn't print every single song in Grades 1-8, but most of them are here. The book opens with songs of praise and thanks, and winds its way through such topics as God as Creator, Protector, and Lord . . . to God's commandments and covenant with his people . . . to our commitment to and love for the Church and other persons . . . to Bible history and characters . . . and full circle to rejoicing in Jesus' life and resurrection.

The usefulness of this book is as wide as your imagination and as versatile as your needs. Four indices—alphabetical, curriculum location, topical, and cassette tape—provide helpful listings of songs found in the book and also in other grade levels and materials. In keeping with the strong Anabaptist tradition of *a cappella* singing, most of the 134 songs are printed with melody and chord symbols. Guitar or autoharp will enhance these tunes. Keyboard accompaniment music is printed for about 40 songs. Every effort has been made to keep the printed music compatible with the versions sung on the demonstration cassette tapes in the teaching packets. You will, therefore, find some differences between music printed in the curriculum and those same songs printed here.

So, sing and be glad! Enjoy finding many songs, formerly scattered throughout various teaching materials, now all in one place. Sing the songs in Sunday school assemblies, club gatherings, children's choirs, worship experiences, and family devotions. Sing about Jesus, the foundation of our faith; learn more about God; and be glad!

The Publishers

1 A Gladsome Hymn of Praise

Ambrose N. Blatchford

Composer unknown
Arr. by Harold Moyer

1. A glad-some hymn of praise we sing, And thank-ful-ly we gath - er To bless the love of God a - bove, Our ev - er - last - ing Fa - ther.
2. Full in his sight his chil - dren stand, By his strong arm de - fend - ed, And he whose wis - dom guides the world, Our foot - steps hath at - tend - ed. In him re - joice with heart and voice whose glo - ry fad - eth nev - er, whose
3. Then praise the Lord with one ac - cord, To his great name give glo - ry, And of his nev - er chang - ing love Re - peat the won - drous sto - ry.

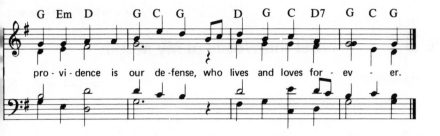

pro - vi - dence is our de -fense, who lives and loves for - ev - er.

Grades 3/4 Year I Quarter 4

God's Love Eternal

2

From the German

Old German melody

Verses

1 God's love e - ter - nal planned my re - demp - tion. God's bound-less
2 I was in bond - age, sin, death, and dark - ness; God's love was
3 God's love sent Je - sus, the faith - ful Sav - ior, to seek and
4 I shall in - her - it e - ter - nal pleas - ure, through Christ in -
5 Thus I am prais - ing God's love e - ter - nal, for aye a -

mer - cy sought e - ven me!
work - ing to make me free.
save me from sin and death. There-fore re - joice and praise his bound-less
her - it e - ter - nal rest.
dor - ing my Sav - ior King.

mer - cy; his love e - ter - nal saves e - ven me!

From *Music Reader for Lutheran Schools.* Copyright © 1933 Concordia Publishing House. Used by permission.

3   Let the Words of My Mouth

Psalm 19:14

Adolph Baumbach, 1862

Let the words of my mouth and the med-i-ta-tions of my heart be ac-cept-a-ble in Thy sight, O Lord, my strength and my Re-deem-er. A-men.

4   Father I Adore You

(A Round)

T. C.

Terry Coelho

Fa-ther I a-dore you, lay my life be-fore you, how I love you.

2 Jesus I adore . . .   3 Spirit I adore . . .

On the demonstration tape, the song is performed in A♭ Major. The singers have adapted the song to group use by changing "I" to "we," "my" to "our," and "life" to "lives."

I Will Sing, I Will Sing

5

Max Dyer

1 I will sing, I will sing a song ___ un - to the Lord. I will

Chorus Al - le - lu, Al - le - lu - ia, glo - ry to the Lord. Al - le -

sing, I will sing a song ___ un - to the Lord. I will sing, I will sing a song

lu, al - le - lu - ia, glo - ry to the Lord. Al - le - lu, al - le - lu - ia, glo -

___ un - to the Lord. Al - le - lu - ia, glo - ry to the Lord.

ry to the Lord. Al - le - lu - ia, glo - ry to the Lord.

2 We will come, we will come as one before
the Lord.
Alleluia, glory to the Lord.

3 If the Son, if the Son shall make you free,
you shall be free indeed.

4 They that sow in tears shall reap in joy.
Alleluia, glory to the Lord.

5 Ev'ry knee shall bow and ev'ry tongue
confess
that Jesus Christ is Lord.

6 In his name, in his name we have the
victory.
Alleluia, glory to the Lord.

This note is sung as a G on the demonstration tape. Only verses 1, 2, and 5 are sung on the cassette.

This song is most effectively sung without any instrumental accompaniment, but with light clapping (finger tips of one hand on palm of another).

Suggested rhythm: | ♩ ♫ ♩ ♫ |

6 Praise and Thanksgiving

Verse 1, tr. Edith L. Thomas
Verse 2, Lester Hostetler

Alsatian round

1 Praise and thanks - giv - ing let ev - 'ry - one bring
2 Praise we the Fa - ther by whom we are fed.

Un - to our Fa - ther for ev - 'ry good thing.
Thank him for giv - ing us dai - ly our bread.

All to - geth - er joy - ful - ly sing!
Praise him, praise him, praise him for bread!

Sung in E Major on the demonstration tape.

Verse 1 from *The Whole World Singing* by Edith Lovell Thomas, © 1950 Friendship Press. Used by permission. Chords symbols added.

7 O, Give Thanks

M. P.

Marion Preheim

O give thanks to the Lord, for he is good. For his stead-fast love en-dures for-ev-er.

Thanks to God

8

From the Portuguese
by Antonio de Campos Goncalves

Brazilian folk song

1 In the morn - ing when I wa - ken, As I
2 When at night the stars are shin - ing, Man - y

kneel and make my prayer, I give thanks to God, the
chil - dren far and near, Talk with God and ask his

Fa - ther, For his ten - der love and care.
bless - ing, Sleep in peace and know no fear.

The melody comes from the central section of the country and was the first folk tune to be used in the New Evangelical Hymn Book of Brazil.

From *The Whole World Singing* by Edith Lovell Thomas, Friendship Press, 1950. Used by permission.

9 Sing, Sing, Praise and Sing

E. S.

Elizabeth Syré

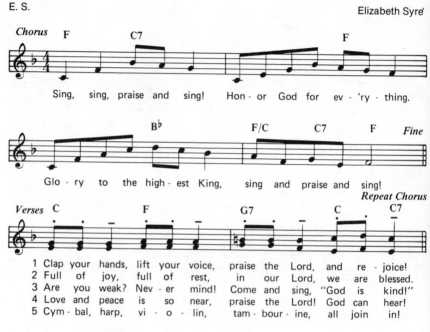

Chorus

Sing, sing, praise and sing! Hon - or God for ev - 'ry - thing.

Glo - ry to the high - est King, sing and praise and sing!

Fine

Repeat Chorus

Verses

1 Clap your hands, lift your voice, praise the Lord, and re - joice!
2 Full of joy, full of rest, in our Lord, we are blessed.
3 Are you weak? Nev - er mind! Come and sing, "God is kind!"
4 Love and peace is so near, praise the Lord! God can hear!
5 Cym - bal, harp, vi - o - lin, tam - bour - ine, all join in!

Copyright by Elizabeth Syré, South Africa. Permission applied for.

10 Thank You, Loving Father

Arthur W. Gross

Ernestine Huber

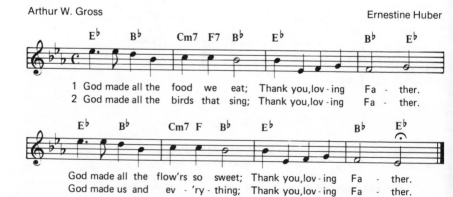

1 God made all the food we eat; Thank you, lov - ing Fa - ther.
2 God made all the birds that sing; Thank you, lov - ing Fa - ther.

God made all the flow'rs so sweet; Thank you, lov - ing Fa - ther.
God made us and ev - 'ry - thing; Thank you, lov - ing Fa - ther.

Father, We Thank Thee

11

Rebecca J. Weston, late 19th century

Dwight Thomas

Fa - ther, we thank thee for the night, And for the pleas- ant
Help us to do the things we should, To be to oth - ers

morn - ing light, for rest and food and lov - ing care, And
kind and good; In all we do at work or play, To

all that makes the day so fair. Fa - ther, we thank thee.
grow more lov - ing ev - er - y day A - men.

Music copyright © 1980 by Dwight Thomas. Used by permission.

Preschool Year II Quarter 4
Grades 1/2 Year I Quarter 1

Thank You, God

12

R. F. S.

Ruth Folta Snogren

Thank you, God, thank you God, For your love and care;

Thank you, God, thank you, God, your love is ev - ery-where.

Words (adapted) and music copyright © 1958 by W. L. Jenkins; from *Songs for Early Childhood at Church and Home.*
Adapted and used by permission of the Westminster Press.

13

Hallelujah

Palestinian folk melody

Hal - le - lu - jah, hal - le - lu - jah, hal - le - lu - jah, hal - le - lu!

Hal - le - lu - jah, hal - le - lu - jah, hal - le - lu - jah, hal - le - lu!

Hal - le - lu - jah, hal - le - lu! Hal - le - lu - jah, hal - le - lu!

Hal - le - lu - jah, hal - le - lu - jah, hal - le - lu - jah, hal - le - lu!

From *The Good Times Songbook*, edited by James Leisy. Abingdon Press, 1974.

14

Song of Praise

T. C. E.
Based on Exodus 15:1-18

Theresa C. Eshbach

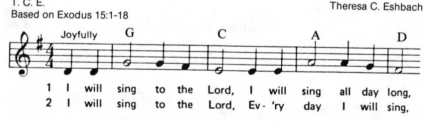

1 I will sing to the Lord, I will sing all day long,
2 I will sing to the Lord, Ev - 'ry day I will sing,

For the Lord is my strength, The Lord is my song.
Let the world hear my song: The Lord God is King.

Rejoice in the Lord Always

(A Round)

15

Philippians 4:4

Source unknown

Re - joice in the Lord__ al - ways; a - gain I say, Re - joice.

Re - joice in the Lord__ al - ways; a - gain I say, Re - joice.

Re - joice; re - joice; a - gain I say, Re - joice.

Re - joice, re - joice; a - gain I say, Re - joice.

Alleluia

16

Traditional

Traditional melody

1 Al - le - lu - ia, al - le - lu - ia, Al - le - lu - ia, Al - le - lu - ia,
2 He's my Sav - ior, He's my Sav - ior, He's my Sav - ior, He's my Sav - ior,

Al - le - lu - ia, al - le - lu - ia, Al - le - lu - ia, al - le - lu - ia!
He's my Sav - ior, He's my Sav - ior, He's my Sav - ior, Al - le - lu - ia!

3 He is worthy . . . 4 I will praise him . . . 5 I will serve him . . .

An unlimited number of additional stanzas are in current use, or may be devised to suit the mood of the occasion.

Variations of this drum rhythm may be added:

17

Psalm 122

(I Rejoiced When I Heard Them Say)

Betty Pulkingham

18 Rejoice, Ye Pure in Heart

Edward Hayes Plumptre, 1865

Arthur Henry Messiter, 1883

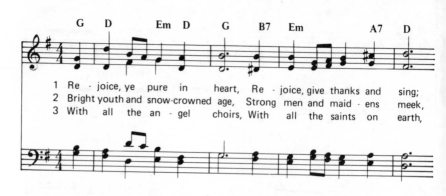

1 Re - joice, ye pure in heart, Re - joice, give thanks and sing;
2 Bright youth and snow-crowned age, Strong men and maid - ens meek,
3 With all the an - gel choirs, With all the saints on earth,

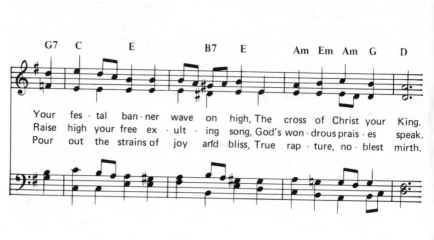

Your fes - tal ban - ner wave on high, The cross of Christ your King.
Raise high your free ex - ult - ing song, God's won - drous prais - es speak.
Pour out the strains of joy and bliss, True rap - ture, no - blest mirth.

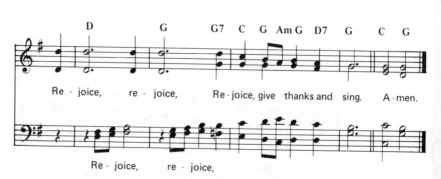

Re - joice, re - joice, Re - joice, give thanks and sing. A - men.

Re - joice, re - joice,

The Big "G" Stands for . . . (Psalm 47) 19

B. C.

Bill Comeau

♩ = 104

Clap your hands, good peo-ple, Sing for joy, good peo-ple. The Lord is

King, good peo-ple. The Lord is King ____ of ev - 'ry-thing. Ev-'ry-bod-y

shout, good peo - ple. Let the prais-es ring, good peo-ple. Let the trum-pets

sing, good peo-ple. The Lord is King ____ of ev - 'ry - thing.

Ev - 'ry wo - man, ev - 'ry man, Ev - 'ry child in ev - 'ry land,
Sum-mer, win-ter, au - tumn, spring, Day and night let prais - es ring,

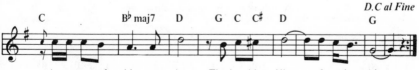

Is a part of his great plan. The Lord is King ___ of ev - 'ry - thing. ___
Un-til the ver - y seas do sing, The Lord is King ___ of ev - 'ry - thing. ___

Music and lyrics from THE BIG "G" STANDS FOR . . . by Bill Comeau, © 1968 by Vanguard Music Corporation, 1595 Broadway, New York, N.Y. 10019. Used by permission.

20   I Sing the Mighty Power of God

Isaac Watts

Adapted from *Gesangbuch*
Württemberg, 1784

1 I sing the_ might - y power of God, that made_ the moun-tains
2 I sing the_ good - ness of the Lord, that filled_ the earth with
3 There's not a plant or flower be - low, But makes_thy glo - ries

rise. That spread the __ flow - ing seas a - broad, And
food; He formed the __ crea - tures with his Word, And
known; And clouds a - rise and tem - pests blow, By

built_ the lof - ty skies. I __ sing the wis - dom
then_ pro - nounced them good. Lord,_ how thy won - ders
or - der from thy throne; While _ all that bor - rows

that or - dained The_ sun to rule the day; The
are dis - played, Where - 'er I turn my eye; If
life from thee Is __ ev - er in thy care, And

moon shines_ full at his com-mand, And all __ the stars o - bey.
I sur - vey the ground I tread, Or gaze_ up - on the sky!
ev - 'ry - where that man can be, thou, God,_ art pres - ent there.

Holy, Holy, Holy

21

Words and music by
Joseph Wise

These measures have been altered by permission from the version in the Grades 3/4 materials to conform with the performance on the demonstration tape.

22 God Is Working His Purpose Out

Arthur Campbell Ainger, 1894   Martin Shaw, 1931

1 God is work-ing his pur-pose out As year suc-
2 From ut-most east to ut-most west, Wher - e'er our
3 March we forth in the strength of God, With the ban-ner of
4 All we can do is noth-ing worth Un - less God

Octaves to the end

ceeds to year: God is work-ing his
feet have trod, By the mouth of man - y
Christ un - furled, That the light of the glo - rious
bless - es the deed; Vain - ly we hope for the

pur-pose out, And the time is draw-ing near: _____ Near - er and
mes-sen - gers Goes forth the voice of God; _____ Give ear to
gos- pel of truth May shine through-out the world: _____ Fight we the
har-vest - tide Till God gives life to the seed; Yet near - er and

near - er draws the time, The time that shall sure-ly be,
me, ye con - ti - nents, Ye isles, give ear to me,
fight with sor-row and sin To set their cap - tives free,
near - er draws the time, The time that shall sure-ly be,

When the earth shall be filled with the glo - ry of God
That the earth may be filled with the glo - ry of God
That the earth may be filled with the glo - ry of God
When the earth shall be filled with the glo - ry of God

1-3   4

As the wa-ters cov-er the sea.   sea.

*The third verse is sung on the demonstration tape in canon, with the second part beginning
at the second measure. Notice that the bass notes in the accompaniment are in canon also.

Tune PURPOSE from *Enlarged Songs of Praise* by permission of Oxford University Press.

23   Miriam's Song

Exodus 15:21   Traditional

The three sections may be sung in various orders (as on the demonstration tape), as a round, or in other combinations.

Come, Thou Almighty King

24

Unknown

Felice De Giardini, 1716-1796

25 Holy, Holy, Holy, Lord God Almighty

Reginald Heber, 1826   John Bacchus Dykes, 1861

1 Ho - ly, ho - ly, ho - ly! Lord God Al - might - y!
2 Ho - ly, ho - ly, ho - ly! All the saints a - dore thee,
3 Ho - ly, ho - ly, ho - ly! Though the dark - ness hide thee,
4 Ho - ly, ho - ly, ho - ly! Lord God Al - might - y!

Ear - ly in the morn - ing our song shall rise to thee;
Cast - ing down their gold - en crowns a - round the glass - y sea;
Though the eye of sin - ful man thy glo - ry may not see;
All thy works shall praise thy name, in earth, and sky, and sea;

Ho - ly, ho - ly, ho - ly! Mer - ci - ful and might - y!
Cher - u - bim and ser - a - phim fall - ing down be - fore thee,
On - ly thou art ho - ly; there is none be - side thee
Ho - ly, ho - ly, ho - ly! Mer - ci - ful and might - y!

God in three per - sons, bless - ed Trin - i - ty!
Which wert, and art, and ev - er - more shalt be.
Per - fect in power, in love, and pur - i - ty.
God in three per - sons, bless - ed Trin - i - ty! A - men.

Old Hundredth

(All People That On Earth Do Dwell)

26

William Kethe, 1561
From Psalm 100

Louis Bourgeois, 1510-1561

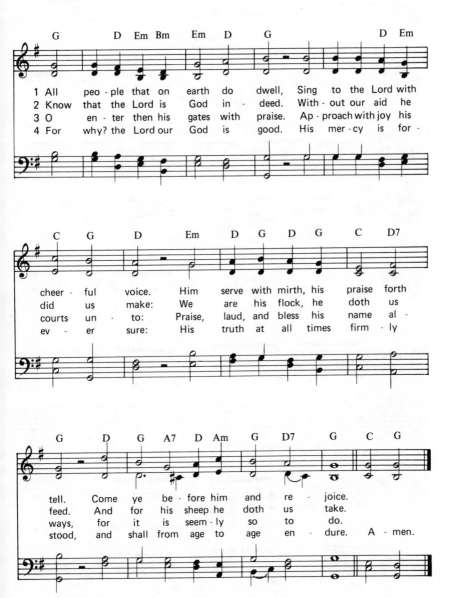

27 We See the Lord

Isaiah 6:1

Source unknown
Arr. by Betty Carr Pulkingham

He is high. an - gels cry, "Ho - ly" The

train fills the tem - ple. The an - gels cry, "Ho - ly," The

an - gels cry, "Ho - ly," The an-gels cry, "Ho-ly is the Lord."____

an-gels cry, "Ho - ly," The an-gels cry, "Ho-ly is the Lord."____

Grades 1/2 Year II Quarter 1

Autumn

28

Ida F. Leyda

Helen M. Browne

1 Ap - ples mel - low, Pump - kins yel - low, Tell the time of year;
2 Col - ors gai - ly, Chang - ing dai - ly, Bright - en field and wood;

Nuts are fall - ing, Na - ture call - ing, Au - tumn time is here.
Au - tumn's glo - ry Tells the sto - ry, God is great and good.

Chords in second line correspond to the demonstration tape version, but not to the student guide.

Used by permission of Emma S. Dietz.

29 For the Beauty of the Earth

Folliott S. Pierpoint   Conrad Kocher

1 For the beau-ty of the earth, For the beau-ty of the skies,
2 For the beau-ty of each hour Of the day and of the night,
3 For the joy of hu-man love, Broth-er, sis-ter, par-ent, child,

For the love which from our birth O-ver and a-round us lies:
Hill and vale, and tree and flower, Sun and moon, and stars of light:
Friends on earth, and friends a-bove; For all gen-tle thoughts and mild:

Lord of all, to thee we raise this our hymn of grate-ful praise.

This Is the Day

30

Les Garrett
Arr. by Dwight Thomas

31 The Butterfly Song

Brian Howard

32   This Is My Father's World

Maltbie D. Babcock
Stanza 3 by Mildred Schell, 1970

Franklin L. Sheppard

1 This is my Fa-ther's world, and__ to my list-'ning ears, all na-ture sings, and__ round me rings the mu-sic of the__ spheres.
2 This is my Fa-ther's world, the__ birds their car-ols raise, the morn-ing light, the__ lil-y white, de-clare their Mak-er's__ praise.
3 This is my Fa-ther's world, in __ cit-y streets and marts, all peo-ple there are__ in his care, he lives with-in their__ hearts.

This is my Fa-ther's world: I __ rest me in the thought of __ rocks and trees, of__ skies and seas; his hand__the won-ders __wrought.
This is my Fa-ther's world: He__ shines in all that's fair; in the rus-tling grass I __ hear him pass, he speaks__to me ev-'ry-where.
This is my Fa-ther's world, when__ peo-ple live as friends, and__ ev-'ry man may__ share His plan, of love__ that nev-er __ ends.

Verses 1 and 2 courtesy of Charles Scribner's Sons. Verse 3 from *Everyone Is Special* by Mildred Schell. Used by permission of Judson Press.

I Love God's Tiny Creatures

33

G. W. Briggs (1875-1959)　　　　　　　　　　　Gordon Slater (1896-1979)

1 I love God's ti - ny crea - tures That wan - der wild and free,
2 Dear Fa - ther, who hast all things made, And car - est for them all,

The cor - al coat - ed la - dy - bird, The vel - vet hum - ming bee;
There's none too great for thy great love, Nor an - y - thing too small:

Shy lit - tle flowers in hedge and dyke That hide them-selves a - way:
If thou canst spend such ten - der care On things that grow so wild,

God paints them, though they are so small, God makes them bright and gay.
How won - der - ful thy love must be For me, thy lov - ing child.

Tune from *Enlarged Songs of Praise* by permission of Oxford University Press. Text from *Songs of Praise for Boys and Girls* by permission of Oxford University Press.

34 Children of the Heavenly Father

Caroline V. Sandell Berg, 1858
Tr. by Ernst William Olson, d. 1958

Swedish melody

1 Chil-dren of the heav'n-ly Fa-ther safe-ly in his bos-om gath-er;
2 Nei-ther life nor death shall ev-er from the Lord his chil-dren sev-er;
3 Though he giv-eth or he tak-eth, God his chil-dren ne'er for-sak-eth,

Nest-ling bird nor star in heav-en such a ref-uge e'er was giv-en.
Un-to them his grace he show-eth, and their sor-rows all he know-eth.
His the lov-ing pur-pose sole-ly to pre-serve them pure and ho-ly.

Text copyright Board of Publication of the Lutheran Church in America. Reprinted by permission.

35 I Will Not Be Afraid

(Tune: Duntroon)

G. E. M. G.

G. E. M. Govan

1 I will_not be a-fraid. __   I will_ not be a-fraid. __
2 He says_ he will be with me.   He says_ he will be with me.
3 His arms_ are un-der-neath me.   His arms_are un-der-neath me.
4 His word_will stand for-ev-er.   His word_will stand for-ev-er.
5 He will_give grace and glo-ry.   He will_give grace and glo-ry.

Words and music used by permission of E. Govan.

I will look up - ward,_ and trav - el on - ward, and not be a - fraid.
He goes be - fore me,_ and is be - side me, so I'm not a - fraid.
His hand up - holds me,_ his love en - folds me, so I'm not a - fraid.
His truth it shall be _ my shield and buck - ler, so I'm not a - fraid.
His cross be - fore me,_ his ban - ner o'er me, so I'm not a - fraid.

Only verses 1, 2, and 5 are included on the demonstration tape.

Grades 1/2 Year II Quarter 4

The Lord Has Children All Around   **36**

(Tune: The Happy Wanderer)

Mary Fretz   Frederich Moller

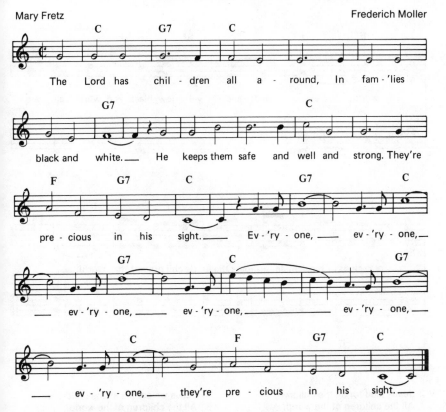

The Lord has chil - dren all a - round, In fam - 'lies

black and white. __ He keeps them safe and well and strong. They're

pre - cious in his sight. __ Ev - 'ry - one, __ ev - 'ry - one, __

__ ev - 'ry - one, __ ev - 'ry - one, __ ev - 'ry - one, __

__ ev - 'ry - one, __ they're pre - cious in his sight. __

Tune "The Happy Wanderer" (Val De Ri-Val De Ra), words by Antonia Ridge, music by Frederich Moller, copyright © MCMLIV by Bosworth and Co. Ltd., London for all countries. All rights for the United States and Canada assigned to: Sam Fox Publishing Co., Inc., New York, New York. All rights reserved. Used by permission. Text copyright © 1979 by Evangel Press, Nappanee, IN 46550; Faith and Life Press, Newton, KS 67114; Mennonite Publishing House, Scottdale, PA 15683.

37 Jesus Loves the Little Children

(Jesus Loves the Children of the World)

C. H. Woolston

George F. Root

1 Je - sus loves the lit - tle chil - dren, all the chil - dren of the

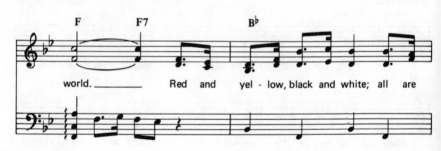

world. _____ Red and yel - low, black and white; all are

pre - cious in his sight. Je - sus loves the lit - tle chil - dren of the world. _____

2 Jesus died for all the children,
All the children of the world,
English, Irish, German, Jew,
Swiss, Dutch, Puerto Rican, too.
Jesus died for all the children of the
world.

3 Jesus welcomes all the children,
All the children of the world,
Black, Hispanic, Indian, white,
Hair that's dark or hair that's light,
Jesus welcomes all the children of the
world.

Song About Jesus and the Children **38**

(Tune: Jesus Loves the Little Children)

Mary Fretz   George F. Root

1 Jesus loves the little children,
All the children here today.
He loves John and Ruth and you,
Mary, Sam, and Judy, too.
He is happy you are here with us today.

2 We will help the little children,
Little children near or far.
We will bring our gifts of love,
Help them learn of God above,
For we love the little children near or far.

Grades 5/6 Year II Quarter 1

Jesus Cares for His People **39**

(Tune: Let Us Break Bread Together)

Anne Neufeld Rupp   American folk hymn

The version printed here is compatible with the demonstration tape, but is different from the printed curriculum.

40 All Night, All Day

Chorus   Spiritual

1 Day is dy - in' in ___ the west, An - gels
2 Now I lay me down ___ to sleep, An - gels
3 Thy love stay with me thru' the night, An - gels

watch - in' o - ver me, my Lord. ___ Sleep, my child, and
watch - in' o - ver me, my Lord. ___ Pray the Lord my
watch - in' o - ver me, my Lord. And wake me with the

take ___ your rest, An - gels watch - in' o - ver me.
soul ___ to keep, An - gels watch - in' o - ver me.
morn - ing light, An - gels watch - in' o - ver me.

41 They That Wait
(Teach Me, Lord, to Wait)

Isaiah 40:31   Stuart Hamblen

They that wait up - on the Lord ___ shall re - new their strength; ___ they shall

mount up with wings as ea-gles; ___ they shall run and not be wea-ry; they shall walk and not faint. ___ Teach me, Lord; teach me, Lord, to wait. ___

Rhythms and notes have been altered from the Grades 7/8 materials to conform with the performance on the demonstration tape.

Grades 5/6 Year I Quarter 3

John 3:16

42

Dwight Thomas

For __ God so loved the world that he gave his on-ly be - got-ten Son __ that __ who - so - ev - er be - liev - eth in him ___ should not per - ish __ but have ev - er - last - ing life, ___ have ev - er - last - ing life. ___

43 Let the Children
(Come to Me)

Mark 10:14

Patricia Shelly

Let the chil - dren come to me, for to such be - longs the king - dom of God. Let the chil - dren come to me, for to such be - longs the king - dom of God.

*These measures are sung with even quarter notes on the demonstration tape.

44 Whoever Calls on the Name of the Lord

Acts 2:21

Patricia Shelly

Who-ev - er calls on the name of the Lord, the name of the Lord, the name of the Lord; Who - ev - er calls on the name of the Lord shall be saved, shall be saved.

God Loves the Children

(Tune: Jesus Loves Me)

45

Mary Fretz

William B. Bradbury, 1816-1868

God made us and all our friends, near or far in oth - er lands.

God knows ev - 'ry lan - guage, too. He cares what we say and do.

God loves the chil - dren, God loves the chil - dren,

God loves the chil - dren, he loves us ev - 'ry - one.

Jesus Loves Me (Spanish)

46

(sung to the tune above)

Cristo me ama, bien lo sé,
Pues la Biblia dice así;
Pesde el cielo él me ve,
Y me dice ven a mí.

Chorus:
Cristo me ama: Cristo me ama;
Cristo me ama; La Biblia dice así.

47 Yo Tengo un Amigo

Tr. Gloria Miller

Source unknown

1 Yo ten-go un a-mi-go que me a-ma, me a-
2 Yo ten-go un ma-es-tro que me en-se-ña, me en-se-
1 I have a true friend who real-ly loves me, he loves___
2 I have a teach-er who is teach-ing me, teaching me,___

ma, me a-ma. Yo ten-go un a-mi-go que me
ña, me en-se-ña. Yo ten-go un ma-es-tro que me en-
me, he loves___ me. I have a true friend who real-ly
teaching me.___ I have a teach-er who is teach-ing

a-ma, su nom-bre es Je-sús.___ Que me
se-ña, su nom-bre es Je-sús.___ Que me en-
loves me, his name is Je-sus Christ.___ Who___
me, ___ his name is Je-sus Christ.___ Who___

a ma, que me a-ma, que me a-ma
se-ña, que me en-se-ña, que me en-se-ña
loves me, who___ loves me, who___ loves me
teaches me, who___ teaches me, who___ teach-es

es mi Sal-va-dor.___ Que me a-ma, que me
es mi Sal-va-dor.___ Que me en-se-ña, que me en-
is___ my___ Lord.___ Who___ loves___ me, who___
is___ my___ Lord.___ Who___ teach-es me, who___

a-ma, su nom-bre es Je-sús.___
se-ña, su nom-bre es Je-sús.___
loves___ me, his name is Je-sus Christ.___
teach-es me, his name is Je-sus Christ.___

Some rhythms and notes have been altered from the version in the Grades 3/4 printed curriculum to conform with the performance on the demonstration tape.

Santa Biblia

48

P. Castro

Melodia Española

1 San - ta Bi - blia, pa - ra mí   E - res un te - so - ro a - quí;
2 Tú re - pren - des mi du - dar;   Tú me ex - hor - tas sin ce - sar;
3 E - res in - fa - li - ble voz   Del Es - pí - ri - tu de Dios
4 Por tu san - ta le - tra sé   Que con Cris - to rei - na - ré

Tú con - tie - nes con ver - dad   La di - vi - na vo - lun - tad;
E - res fa - ro que a mi pie,   Va gui - an - do por la fe;
Que vi - gor al al - ma da   Cuan - do en a - flic - ción es - tá;
Yo que tan in - dig - no soy,   Por tu luz al cie - lo voy;

Tú me di - ces lo que soy,   De quien vi - ne y a quien voy.
A las fuen - tes del a - mor   Del ben - di - to Sal - va - dor.
Tú me en - se - ñas a triun - far   De la muer - te y el pe - car.
San - ta Bi - blia, pa - ra mí   E - res un te - so - ro a - quí. A - mén.

Recorded on the teaching cassette in the key of D, last verse in E.

English translation:

1 Holy Bible, you to me, are a treasure here below. / You contain most certainly God's divine will for me; / You enlighten who I am; Where I'm going and where I'm from.

2 You correct my nagging doubt; You teach me what God's about; / You're a light unto my feet, gently guide me in my faith / To the fountain of the love of the blessed Savior's heart.

3 You are the unfailing voice of the Spirit, God's own choice; / You give strength unto my soul when affliction takes its toll; / You instruct me how to win o'er the power of death and sin.

4 By your Holy Word I know that one day with Christ I'll reign; / I who so unworthy am, by your light to heav'n will go; / Holy Bible, you to me, are a treasure here below. / Amen

Translated by Howard Yoder

49 He's Got the Whole World in His Hands

Spiritual

He's got the whole world in his hands; he's got the whole world in his hands; he's got the whole world in his hands; he's got the whole world in his hands.

2 The wind and the rain . . .   3 The tiny little baby . . .
4 you and me, sister . . . you and me, brother . . . everybody . . .

The printed music above corresponds to the Grades 3/4 Year I Quarter 3 demonstration tape. However, the printed versions in Grades 3/4 Year I Quarter 3, and Grades 1/2 Year I Quarter 4 and Year II Quarter 2 resemble the music to "We'll Put Our Faith in Jesus," printed below.

50 We'll Put Our Faith in Jesus

(Variation of the tune, "He's Got the Whole World in His Hands")

Linea Reimer Geiser

Spiritual

We'll put our faith in Je - sus, he'll keep us strong.__ We'll trust each oth - er too,__ as we move a - long.__ We'll put our trust in Je - sus, that's our song.__ He'll lead us to the prom - ised land.

Text copyright © 1978 by Evangel Press, Nappanee, IN 46550; Faith and Life Press, Newton, KS 67114; Mennonite Publishing House, Scottdale, PA 15683.

On Jordan's Stormy Banks **51**

Samuel Stennett, 1787

W. Walter's *Southern Harmony*, 1835
Harmonized by J. Harold Moyer, 1965

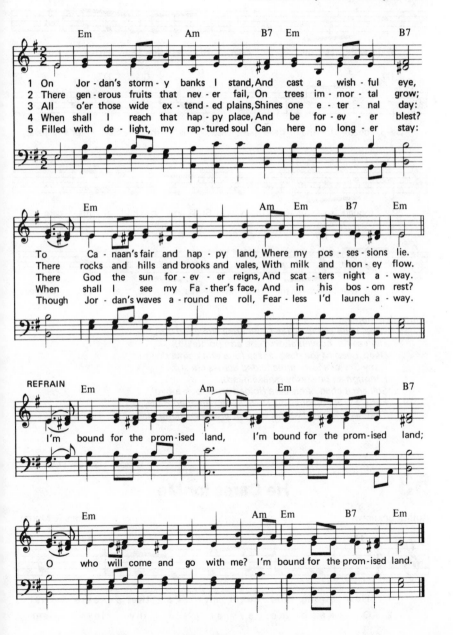

1 On Jor-dan's storm-y banks I stand, And cast a wish-ful eye,
2 There gen-erous fruits that nev-er fail, On trees im-mor-tal grow;
3 All o'er those wide ex-tend-ed plains, Shines one e-ter-nal day:
4 When shall I reach that hap-py place, And be for-ev-er blest?
5 Filled with de-light, my rap-tured soul Can here no long-er stay:

To Ca-naan's fair and hap-py land, Where my pos-ses-sions lie.
There rocks and hills and brooks and vales, With milk and hon-ey flow.
There God the sun for-ev-er reigns, And scat-ters night a-way.
When shall I see my Fa-ther's face, And in his bos-om rest?
Though Jor-dan's waves a-round me roll, Fear-less I'd launch a-way.

REFRAIN

I'm bound for the prom-ised land, I'm bound for the prom-ised land;

O who will come and go with me? I'm bound for the prom-ised land.

52

Wide, Wide As the Ocean

Source unknown

Wide, wide as the o-cean, High as the hea-ven a-bove,
Deep, deep as the deep-est sea is my Sav-ior's love;
I, though so un-worth-y, Still am a child of his care;
For his Word teach-es me that his love reach-es me, ev-'ry-where.

Suggested motions:

Wide, wide as the ocean (both arms stretched out),
High as the heaven above (one arm points up),
Deep, deep as the deepest sea (one arm points down)
Is my Savior's love (arms folded across chest).
I, though so unworthy (shake head),
Still am a child of his care (folded arms rock-a-bye),
For his Word teaches me (hands form an open Bible)
That his love reaches me, everywhere (arms flung out).

53

He Cares for Me

Author unknown

James R. Murray

1 How strong and sweet my Fa-ther's care that
2 O keep me ev-er in thy love, dear

'round   a - bout me, like   the   air,   is
Fa - ther, watch - ing from a - bove,   and

with   me   al - ways, ev - 'ry - where! He   cares   for   me.
as   through life my steps shall move, O   care   for   me.

Grades 1/2 Year II Quarter 3
Grades 3/4 Year II Quarter 3

The Lord Is My Shepherd   **54**

(A Round)

Adapted from Psalm 23   Source unknown

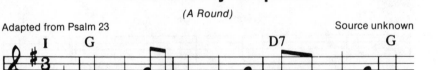

The Lord is   my Shep - herd; I'll walk with him al - way.

He leads by   still wa - ters; I'll walk with him al - way.

Al - way, al - way,   I'll   walk   with   him   al - way.

Al - way, al - way,   I'll   walk   with   him   al - way.

This song is reprinted as found in Grades 3/4 Year II Quarter 3. It is also found in the key of F in Grades 1/2 Year II Quarter 3, teachers guide, p. 64, with slightly different words and rhythm.

55 O Worship the Lord

(A Round)

Adapted from Psalm 100

Dwight Thomas

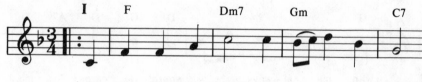

O wor-ship the Lord, for he is our God

and we are his peo-ple, the folk of his pas-ture.

O wor-ship the Lord, our Ma-ker, our God, our God.

56 We're Following the Leader

Theresa C. Eschbach

Source unknown

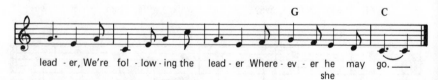

We're fol - low-ing the lead - er, the lead - er, the

lead - er, We're fol - low-ing the lead - er Where - ev - er he may go.
she

Use any actions that the children can easily follow as they sing (e.g. clapping hands, standing on one foot, walking, skipping). Choose a different child to be leader each time you sing.

Whosoever Will

57

Source unknown

Who - so - ev er will to the Lord may come, who-so-ev - er

will to the Lord may come, who - so - ev - er will to the

Lord may come, he'll not turn one a - way. ___

Je - sus, Je - sus, Je - sus, Je - sus, heals the

bro - ken - heart - ed, Je - sus, Je - sus, Je - sus, Je - sus,

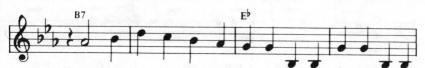

heals the bro - ken - heart - ed, Je - sus, Je - sus, Je - sus, Je - sus,

heals the bro - ken - heart - ed, he will set you free.

58 The New 23rd

Words and music by Ralph Carmichael

59 Obey My Voice

Jeremiah 7:23

Sheilagh Nowacki

Rhythm on demonstration tape:

Grades 5/6 Year I Quarter 2

God Has Spoken

60

W. F. Jabusch

Traditional Israeli folk song

*The words to verse 2 have been printed as sung on the demonstration tape. However, the author now prefers a more inclusive version: "**They** who **have** ears to . . . let **them** hear! . . . **They** who would learn . . . let **them** hear. . . ."*

61 They Shall Be My People

Jeremiah 31:33b-34

Dwight Thomas

I will put my law____ with - in them, ____ and I will

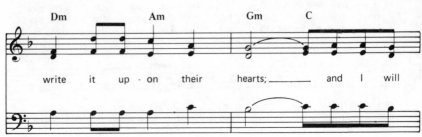

write it up - on their hearts; ____ and I will

be their God, I will be their God, and they shall be my

peo - ple, ____ they shall__ be my peo - ple. ____

Verses

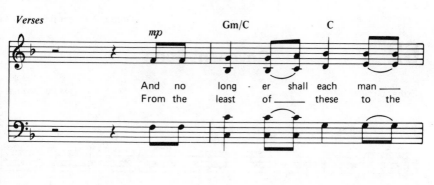

And no long - er shall each man ___
From the least of ___ these to the

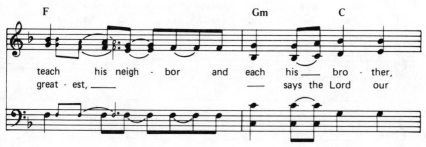

teach his neigh - bor and each his ___ bro - ther,
great - est, ___ ___ says the Lord our

say - ing, ___ "Know the Lord, Know the Lord," ___ for
God; I will for - give their in - iq - ui - ty, and re -

D.C. al Fine

they shall all know me, they shall all know me.
mem - ber their sin no more, re - mem - ber their sin no more.

62

Covenant Song

Esther Groves

Dwight Thomas

We give our - selves to a liv - ing God in
And he will up - hold us with his love for -

cov - e - nant, in cov - e - nant, ev - er -

more. _____ Al - le - lu - ia, A -

le - lu - ia, A - le - lu - ia.

We Love God and Obey His Commandments **63**

Adapted from 1 John 5:2

Patricia Shelly

We love God and o - bey his com - mand - ments, o -
bey his com - mand - ments, o - bey his com - mand - ments.
We love God and o - bey his com - mand - ments.
We are God's chil - dren. He loves us so.

I Will Hear **64**

Adapted from Psalm 85:8

Irma C. Collignon

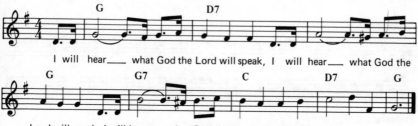

I will hear____ what God the Lord will speak, I will hear____ what God the
Lord will speak, I will hear____ what God the Lord will speak, His voice I'll o - bey.

Obbligato:

65   You Shall Love the Lord Your God

Edna Dyck
Based on Deut. 6:4-5

Joan Wiebe

1 Chil - dren of the Bi - ble Of - ten heard these words. They
2 Ruth who was a stran - ger Came to Beth - le - hem. God
3 Jo - ash was a young king, Hap - py in his work. He
4 Dan - iel lived in Ba-by-lon, Far from his home-town. He

served him faith - ful - ly each day be - cause they loved the Lord.
gave her friends and hap - pi - ness be - cause she loved the Lord.
helped to make God's tem - ple new be - cause he loved the Lord.
would not eat the king's rich food be - cause he loved the Lord.

You shall love the Lord, your God. You shall love the Lord, your God. The

Lord your God is — one — Lord. Love him with all your might.

Instrument 1

Instrument 2

Faith of Our Fathers

66

Frederick W. Faber

Henri Frederick Hemy
adapted by James G. Walton

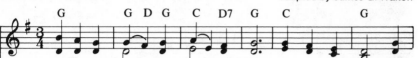

1 Faith of our fa - thers, liv - ing still In spite of dun - geon,
2 Our fa-thers, chained in pris - ons dark, Were still in heart and
3 Faith of our fa - thers, we will love Both friend and foe in

fire, and sword; O how our hearts beat high with joy
con - science free: How sweet would be their chil - dren's fate,
all our strife; And preach thee, too, as love knows how,

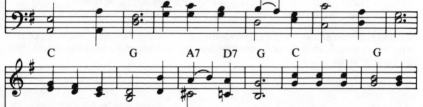

When - e'er we hear that glo - rious word. Faith of our fa - thers,
If they, like them, could die for thee. Faith of our fa - thers,
By kind - ly words and vir - tuous life: Faith of our fa - thers,

ho - ly faith. We will be true to thee till death!
ho - ly faith. We will be true to thee till death!
ho - ly faith. We will be true to thee till death!

67   I Have Decided to Follow Jesus

An Indian prince   Folk melody from India

1 I have de - cid - ed ____ to fol-low Je - sus, ____ I have de -
2 Tho' no one join me, ____ still I will fol - low, ____ Tho' no one
3 The world be - hind me, ____ the cross be - fore me, ____ The world be -

cid - ed ____ to fol-low Je - sus, ____ I have de - cid - ed ____
join me, ____ still I will fol - low, ____ Tho' no one join me ____
hind me, ____ the cross be - fore me, ____ The world be - hind me ____

____ to fol-low Je - sus ____ No turn-ing back, ____ no turn-ing back! ____
____ still I will fol - low ____ No turn-ing back, ____ no turn-ing back! ____
____ the cross be - fore me ____ No turn-ing back, ____ no turn-ing back! ____

A piano arrangement, with slight chord variations, is found in the Grades 5/6 Year I Quarter 3 materials. The Grades 7/8 demonstration tape version includes a key change to D Major on the final verse.

68   We Are Turning God's Way

(Tune: We Are Climbing Jacob's Ladder)

Linea R. Geiser   Traditional

We are turn - ing God's way, God's way. We are turn - ing God's way,

God's way. We are turn - ing God's way, God's way, when we hear him call!

Love, Love

69

Source unknown

Love, love, love, love, the gos-pel in a word is___ love.

Love your neigh-bor as your_ bro - ther. Love, love, love, love. love.
(sis - ter)

This song may be sung as a round, or one group may play or sing the D whole notes while another group sings the melody.

People Need Each Other

70

Florence E. Wagner

German folk song

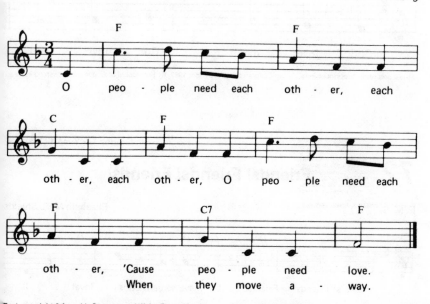

O peo - ple need each oth - er, each

oth - er, each oth - er, O peo - ple need each

oth - er, 'Cause peo - ple need love.
When they move a - way.

Text copyright © from *It's Summer and We're Three.* Used by permission of Judson Press.

71   Hello, Hello! How Are You?

M. P.
Verses 2, 3 adapted for The Foundation Series

Marie Pooler

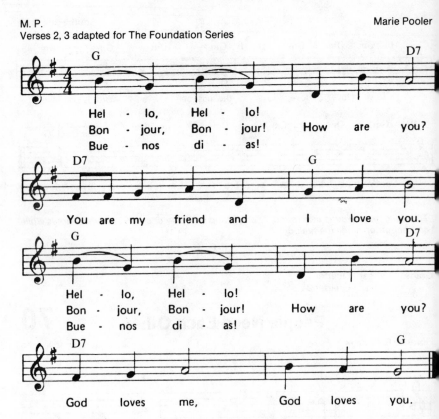

Hel - lo, Hel - lo! How are you?
Bon - jour, Bon - jour! How are you?
Bue - nos di - as!

You are my friend and I love you.

Hel - lo, Hel - lo! How are you?
Bon - jour, Bon - jour! How are you?
Bue - nos di - as!

God loves me, God loves you.

Music and verse 1 reprinted from *Young Children Sing*, copyright 1967, by permission of Augsburg Publishing House.

72   Friends! Friends! Friends!

E. M. S.

Elizabeth McE. Shields

Friends! Friends! Friends! I have some friends I love! I

Permission applied for.

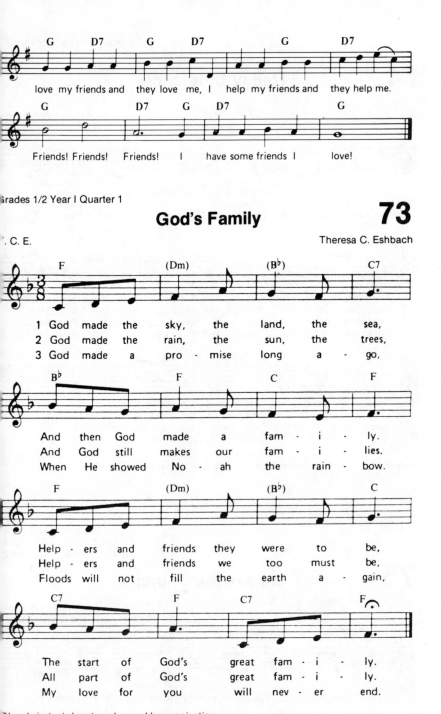

Grades 1/2 Year I Quarter 1

God's Family

73

T. C. E.

Theresa C. Eshbach

Chords in ( ) denote enhanced harmonization.

74   Happy Differences

M. H. A.

Mae Hurley Ashworth

1 Some things are round;___ some things are square;___
2 Food is___ cooked in ma - ny___ ways, And
3 Peo - ple are dark, and peo - ple are fair; They
4 Chil - dren___ wor - ship God and___ pray,

Col - ors are diff - 'rent here and there;___ Snow is ___ cold, and there's
wea - ther chan - ges through the days;___ Find-ing things diff-'rent is
may have straight or cur - ly hair;___ Some are ___ short, and ___
Act and think and talk and play In ma - ny ___ ways, and ___

heat in flame, And oh, what fun that they're not the same!
like a game, And oh, what fun that they're not the same!
some are tall, But oh, what fun to ___ know them all!
oh, what fun To meet and know them ___ ev - 'ry one!

From the filmstrip "Our World of Happy Differences" copyright © 1963 by Friendship Press, New York City, N.Y. Guitar chords added. Used by permission.

Kindergarten Quarter 3
Grades 5/6 Year II Quarter 4
Grades 7/8 Year I Quarter 2

75   We Are the Church

Words and music by
Richard Avery and Donald Marsh

I am the church! You are the church! We are the church to - geth - er!

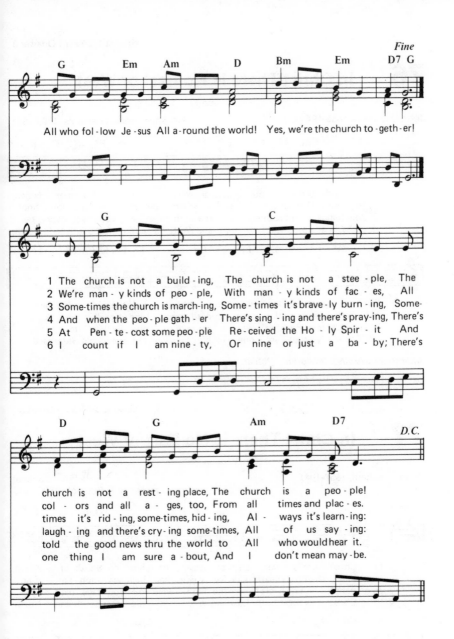

All who fol-low Je-sus All a-round the world! Yes, we're the church to-geth-er!

1 The church is not a build-ing, The church is not a stee - ple, The
2 We're man - y kinds of peo - ple, With man - y kinds of fac - es, All
3 Some-times the church is march-ing, Some - times it's brave-ly burn-ing, Some-
4 And when the peo - ple gath - er There's sing - ing and there's pray-ing, There's
5 At Pen - te - cost some peo-ple Re - ceived the Ho - ly Spir - it And
6 I count if I am nine - ty, Or nine or just a ba - by; There's

church is not a rest - ing place, The church is a peo - ple!
col - ors and all a - ges, too, From all times and plac - es.
times it's rid - ing, some-times, hid - ing, Al - ways it's learn - ing:
laugh - ing and there's cry - ing some-times, All of us say - ing:
told the good news thru the world to All who would hear it.
one thing I am sure a - bout, And I don't mean may - be.

Optional actions found in the Kindergarten Quarter 3 materials:
  "I am the church, you are the church" (Point to self, then to another person)
  "We are the church together" (Two join hands)
  "All who follow Jesus, all around the world" (Spread arms wide)
  "Yes, we're the church together" (Join hands in a circle)

76 In Christ There Is No East or West

(Version 1)

John Oxenham, 1852-1941

Alexander Robert Reinagle, 1799-1877

1 In Christ there is no East or West, In him no South or North;
2 In him shall true hearts ev - 'ry-where their high com - mun-ion find;
3 Join hands, then, broth-ers* of the faith, what-e'er your race may be.
4 In Christ now meet both East and West, In him meet South and North;

But one great fel-low-ship of love through-out the whole wide earth.
His serv-ice is the gold-en cord close bind-ing all man-kind.
Who serves my Fa-ther as a son** is sure-ly kin to me.
All Christ-ly souls are one in him through-out the whole wide earth.

*Alternative wording: *children **child*

77 In Christ There Is No East or West

(Version 2)

John Oxenham, 1852-1941

Spiritual
Adapted by Harry T. Burleigh, 1866-1949

1 In Christ there is no East or West, In him no South or North;
2 In him shall true hearts ev - 'ry-where their high com-mun-ion find;
3 Join hands, then, broth-ers* of the faith, what-e'er your race may be!
4 In Christ now meet both East and West, in him meet South and North,

But one great fel-low-ship of love through-out the whole wide earth.
His serv-ice is the gold-en cord close bind-ing all man-kind.
Who serves my Fa-ther as a son** is sure-ly kin to me.
All Christ-ly souls are one in him, through-out the whole wide earth.

*Alternative wording: *children **child*

The Bond of Love

78

O. S.

Otis Skillings

79 Magic Penny

Words and music by Malvina Reynolds

Chorus

Love is some-thing if you give it a-way,_ give it a-way,_ give it a-way._

Love is some-thing if you give it a-way,_ You end up hav-ing more.

Verse 1

It's just like a mag-ic pen-ny, Hold it tight and you won't have an-y.

Lend it, spend it, and you'll have so man-y, they'll roll all o-ver the floor, for

Chorus

love is some-thing if you give it a-way,_ give it a-way,_ give it a-way,_

love is some-thing if you give it a-way,_ you'll end up hav-ing more. So

Verse 2

let's love ev-'ry-one we meet each day, And show them we know the Je-sus way.

For love is some-thing if you give it a-way,_ you end up hav-ing more.

If you wish to sing the song as it is on the demonstration cassette, repeat the chorus, verse 1, and then twice through the chorus at the end.

Love, Love, Love

80

Herbert F. Brokering

Lois Brokering

1 Love, love, love! That's what it's all a - bout! 'Cause
2 Peace, peace, peace!

God loves us, we love each oth - er, moth - er, fa - ther, sis - ter, broth - er.

Ev - 'ry - bod - y sing and shout, 'cause that's what it's all a - bout! It's a - bout

love, love, love! It's a - bout love, love, love!
peace, peace, peace! It's a - bout peace, peace, peace!

3 Joy, joy, joy . . . 4 Me, me, me . . . 5 You, you, you . . .

81 Let There Be Peace On Earth

(Let It Begin With Me)

By Sy Miller and Jill Jackson

82

Unity

Words and music by Gerald Derstine

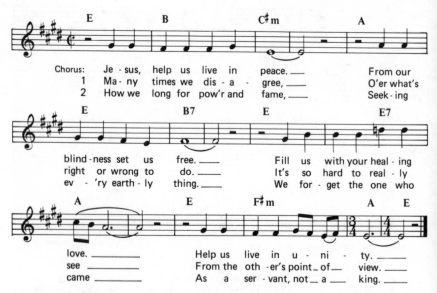

Chorus: Je - sus, help us live in peace. ___ From our
1 Ma - ny times we dis - a - gree, ___ O'er what's
2 How we long for pow'r and fame, ___ Seek - ing

blind - ness set us free. ___ Fill us with your heal - ing
right or wrong to do. ___ It's so hard to real - ly
ev - 'ry earth - ly thing. ___ We for - get the one who

love. ___ Help us live in u - ni - ty. ___
see ___ From the oth - er's point _ of _ view. ___
came ___ As a ser - vant, not _ a _ king. ___

Note values at the ends of lines 1, 2, and 3 have been extended by permission of the composer to conform to the demonstration tape performance.

Copyright © 1971 by Gerald Derstine, 1106 17th Avenue South, Nashville, TN 37212. Used by permission.

83

Make Peace!

B. B.

Beth Berry

1 "I don't like you!" Jim told Jack. So Jack hit him and
2 "You're too boss - y," Sue told Pat. So Pat pinched her and

Jim hit back. They scrapped and ___ fought the whole ___ day through,
said, "You're fat!" They stuck out their tongues and stamped ___ a - way,

Copyright © 1974 by Herald Press, Scottdale, PA 15683. Used by permission.

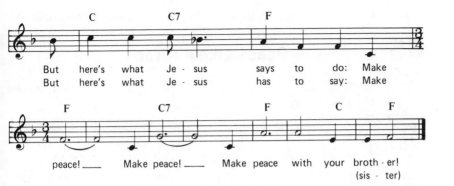

But here's what Je-sus says to do: Make
But here's what Je-sus has to say: Make

peace!___ Make peace!___ Make peace with your broth-er!
(sis - ter)

God's Family

84

P. S.

P. Shelly

Chorus **Lively**

All grown-ups, all chil-dren, all moth-ers, all fath-ers are

sis-ters and broth-ers in the fam-'ly of God.

Verses

1 I am a per-son; God made me spe-cial. You are a
2 So man-y chil-dren, all of them dif-'rent. God gave each
3 God has a fam-'ly with man-y peo-ple: Grown-ups and

per-son and you're spe-cial, too. We have our fam-'lies and
per-son his own thing to do. All of God's chil-dren are
chil-dren who love God to - day. We get to-geth-er to

friends we can play with.___ There are so man-y good things we can do.
sis-ters and broth-ers.___ I know God loves me, and God loves you, too.
care for each oth-er to wor-ship and learn how to fol-low God's way.

85 Peace Like a River

Traditional

1 I've got peace like a riv-er, I've got peace like a
riv-er, I've got peace like a riv-er in my soul, ___
I've got peace like a riv-er, I've got peace like a
riv-er, I've got peace like a riv-er in my soul. ___

2 joy like a fountain . . . 3 love like an ocean . . . 4 peace . . . joy . . . love

86 Offering Song

Author unknown

A. C. Kolb

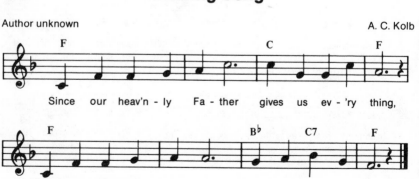

Since our heav'n-ly Fa-ther gives us ev-'ry thing,

Lov-ing-ly and glad-ly, now our gifts we bring.

Breathe on Me, Breath of God **87**

Edwin Hatch

Robert Jackson

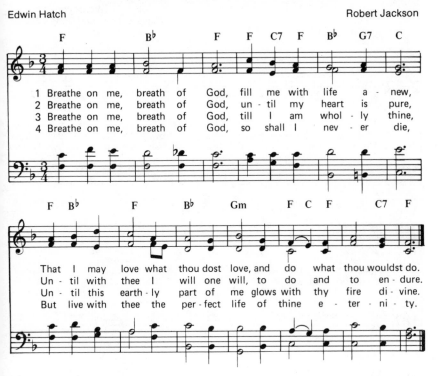

1 Breathe on me, breath of God, fill me with life a - new,
That I may love what thou dost love, and do what thou wouldst do.

2 Breathe on me, breath of God, un - til my heart is pure,
Un - til with thee I will one will, to do and to en - dure.

3 Breathe on me, breath of God, till I am whol - ly thine,
Un - til this earth - ly part of me glows with thy fire di - vine.

4 Breathe on me, breath of God, so shall I nev - er die,
But live with thee the per - fect life of thine e - ter - ni - ty.

Kum Ba Yah **88**

Spiritual

Slowly

Kum ba yah, my Lord, Kum ba yah! Kum ba yah, my Lord, Kum ba yah!

Kum ba yah, my Lord, Kum ba yah! O Lord, Kum ba yah!

2 Someone's crying, Lord, Kum ba yah!   4 Someone's praying, Lord, Kum ba yah!
3 Someone's singing, Lord, Kum ba yah!   5 Come by here, my Lord, Come by here!

89 Passed Thru the Waters

Words and music by
Richard Avery and Donald Marsh

1 Like sur - vi - vors of the Flood, Like walk - ers thru the sea, Like
2 Like small child - ren washed and clean, Or drowned to live a - gain, Like
3 Do you see the Spir - it's fire? And hear the wind blow free? Do you

walk - ers thru the God - di - vid - ed sea: _____ We are
peo - ple drowned and brought to life a - gain: _____ We are
feel the wind and fi - re blow - ing free? _____ We are

res - cued, we are claimed, we are loved and we are named,
washed and we are saved, we are ri - sen from the grave,
cho - sen each by name, marked by wa - ter, then by flame,

Chorus

We are bap - tized! _____ I am bap - tized! _____ We have

passed thru the wa - ters And that's all that mat - ters! We have

passed thru the wa - ters! O thanks be to God!

Grades 1/2 Year II Quarter 3

You Shall Receive Power

90

Acts 1:8

Patricia Shelly

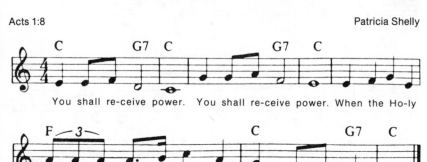

You shall re-ceive power. You shall re-ceive power. When the Ho-ly

Spir - it has come up - on you, you shall re - ceive power.

Recorded on the demonstration tape in the key of D♭.

91 Spirit of God, Unseen as the Wind

(Tune: Skye Boat Song)

M. V. Old

Scottish folk song
Arr. by Alastair Durden, b. 1948

Spir - it of God, un - seen as the wind, gen - tle as is the dove;

teach us the truth and help us be - lieve, show us the Sav - ior's love.

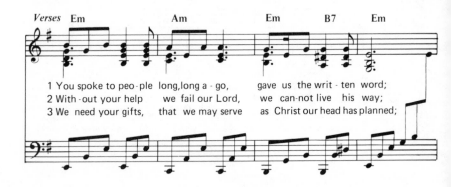

1 You spoke to peo - ple long, long a - go, gave us the writ - ten word;
2 With - out your help we fail our Lord, we can - not live his way;
3 We need your gifts, that we may serve as Christ our head has planned;

we read it still, need-ing its truth, through it God's voice is heard.
we need your power, we need your strength, fol - low-ing Christ each day.
we need your fruit, love, joy and peace, we need your guid - ing hand.

Grades 3/4 Year II Quarter 1
Grades 5/6 Year I Quarter 4

Every Time I Feel the Spirit   92

Spiritual

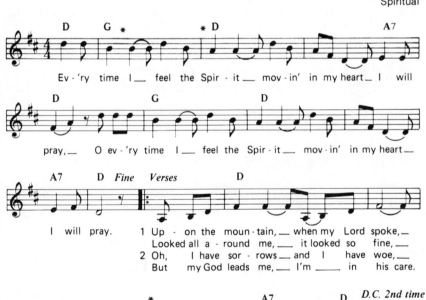

Ev - 'ry time I __ feel the Spir - it __ mov - in' in my heart __ I will

pray, __ O ev - 'ry time I __ feel the Spir - it __ mov - in' in my heart __

I will pray. 1 Up - on the moun - tain, __ when my Lord spoke, __
                  Looked all a - round me, __ it looked so fine, __
                  2 Oh, I have sor - rows __ and I have woe, __
                  But my God leads me, __ I'm __ in his care.

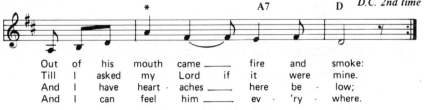

Out of his mouth came ____ fire and smoke:
Till I asked my Lord if it were mine.
And I have heart - aches ____ here be - low;
And I can feel him ____ ev - 'ry - where.

*These measures are sung | ♩ ♩ ♫ | on the Grades 3/4 demonstration tape.

93   It Is the Holy Spirit's Day

Alda M. Milner-Barry   Traditional Cornish melody

1 It is the Ho - ly Spir - it's day, Sing
2 With rush - ing sound, with heav'n - ly flame On

joy - ful al - le - lu - ia! When all Christ's peo - ple
them the Ho - ly Spir - it came: They blessed and praised God's

met to pray; Sing joy - ful al - le - lu - ia!
glo - rious name; Sing joy - ful al - le - lu - ia!

Traditional Cornish melody from *Sing for Joy* by Norman and Margaret Mealy. Copyright © The Seabury Press, Inc., 1961. Used by permission. Text used by permission of St. Christopher's College Trust, The National Society, Church House, Bean's Yard, Westminster London SWIP 3NZ.

94   A Charge to Keep I Have

Charles Wesley, 1762   George Kingsley, 1842

1 A charge to keep I have, A God to glo - ri - fy;
2 To serve the pres - ent age, My call - ing to full - fil,

A nev-er-dy-ing soul to save, And fit it for the sky.
O, may it all my powers en-gage To do my Mas-ter's will!

Additional verses may be found in Hymns for Praise and Worship, *#509,* Hymns of Faith and Life, *#346, and* The Mennonite Hymnal, *#351.*

Grades 7/8 Year I Quarter 1

Heart and Mind, Possessions, Lord 95

Krishnarao Rathnaji Sangle, d. 1908
Tr. by Alden H. Clark, b. 1878, and others

Ancient Indian melody
Adapted by Marion Jean Chute, b. 1901

1 Heart and mind, pos-ses-sions, Lord, I of-fer un-to thee;
2 Heart and mind, pos-ses-sions, Lord, I of-fer un-to thee;

All these were thine, Lord;__ thou didst give them all to me.
Thou art the way, the __ truth; __ thou __ art the life.

Won-drous are thy do-ings un-to me. Plans __ and my thoughts and
Sin-ful, I com-mit my-self to thee. Je-sus Christ is fill-ing

ev-'ry-thing I ev-er do are de-pend-ent on thy __
all __ the __ heart of me. He can give me vic-t'ry o'er

will __ and love a-lone. I com-mit my spir-it un-to thee.
all __ that threat-ens me. Je-sus Christ is fill-ing all my heart.

96   We've a Story to Tell to the Nations

H. Ernest Nichol (Colin Sterne), 1862-1928

Adapted from H. Ernest
Nichol, 1862-1928

Christ's great king-dom shall come on earth, The king-dom of love and light.

Grades 5/6 Year II Quarter 1

There Were Twelve

97

A. N. R.

A. N. Rupp

There were twelve dis - ci - ples, Je - sus chose to be a - pos - tles:

Si - mon Pe - ter, An - drew, James and his broth - er John,

Phil - ip, Thom - as, Mat - thew, James, the son of Al - pheus,

Ju - das, son of James, Si - mon, one Bar - tho - lo - mew,

And the one from Ker - i - oth, whose name was Ju - das too:

Twelve dis - ci - ples, twelve a - pos - tles, cho - sen to do the work of God;

Twelve dis - ci - ples, twelve a - pos - tles, cho - sen for the work of God.

98   **Take Up Your Cross**

Luke 9:23

Jerry Derstine and Randy Noe

Use chords in ( ) with autoharp not having E Major chords.

The version printed above has been altered from the version printed in the curriculum so that it is compatible with the demonstration tape.

Day by Day

99

Words and music by
Stephen Schwartz

100   Pass It On

K. K.

Kurt Kaiser

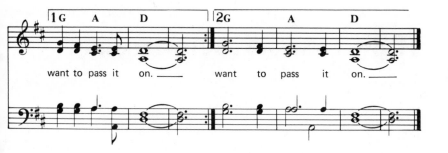

want to pass it on. ____ want to pass it on. ____

Grades 1/2 Year I Quarter 2

And There Were Twelve

101

J. M. and T. C. E.

Jean Moyer and Theresa C. Eshbach

And there were twelve, twelve, twelve dis - ci - ples stand - ing

by his side; Twelve to spread the Good News far and wide;

Twelve dis - ci - ples for our Lord, And I'd like to be one

too to - day; I'd like to be one too.

After listening to the cassette you will notice that rhythm and movement are natural to this song. A coffee-can drum, dried-twig rhythm sticks, and paper-plate tambourines provide a special accompaniment and are a delight to the children.

102   Silver and Gold Have I None

Acts 3:6   Source unknown

Sil-ver and gold have I none, But such as I have give I thee. In the

name of Je - sus Christ of Naz-ar-eth, rise up and walk.

Walk-ing and leap-ing and prais-ing God, Walk-ing and leap-ing and prais-ing God in the

name of Je - sus Christ of Naz-ar-eth, rise up and walk!

103   Good News

Evangelist Abraham Mumol   Native Buzi (Liberian) tune
Text altered   From the Reverend George R. Flora

Recitative style

1 I have heard good news to - day! Who has told
2 Je - sus is the Son of God! Who has told
  Fai - ni ne ye gi me - ni ga! Be ya bo - ga -

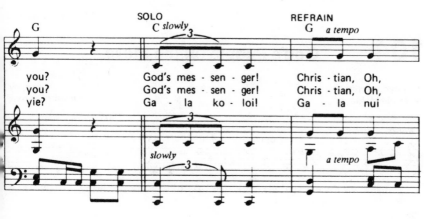

3 **Solo:** Jesus is the Friend of all!
Refrain: Who has told you?
Solo: God's messenger!
Refrain: Christian, Oh, who has told you?
Solo: God's messenger!

This song shows how local customs are adapted to Christian uses. One day a missionary, Mr. Flora, was visiting evangelist Abraham Mumol in Fissibon, when he heard the children singing, clapping their hands, and stamping their feet to mark the rhythm. He learned that they were using the music of a folk song to which had been set the words given above. Drums and rattles are used as the people sing. All consonants are harsh. Short **i** as in **knit**; short **e** as in **get**; long **i** as **ee**; **y** is soft gutteral, like **gh** in **sigh**; diphthong **ai** as **eye**; **oi** as in **boy**.

Printed by permission of Lutheran Church Women, 2900 Queen Lane, Philadelphia, PA 19129-1091.

104 God's People on the Move

Adapted from Acts 7
by Marie M. Moyer

music by
Dwight Thomas

Chorus

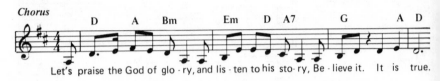

Let's praise the God of glo-ry, and lis-ten to his sto-ry, Be-lieve it. It is true.

Descant

Let's praise the God of glo-ry. Be-lieve it. It is true.

Verses

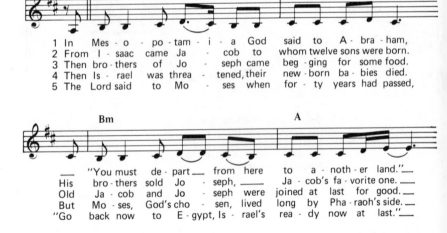

1 In Mes-o-po-tam-i-a God said to A-bra-ham,
2 From I-saac came Ja-cob to whom twelve sons were born.
3 Then bro-thers of Jo-seph came beg-ging for some food.
4 Then Is-rael was threa-tened, their new-born ba-bies died.
5 The Lord said to Mo-ses when for-ty years had passed,

___ "You must de-part ___ from here to a-noth-er land." ___
His bro-thers sold Jo-seph, ___ Ja-cob's fa-vorite one. ___
Old Ja-cob and Jo-seph were joined at last for good. ___
But Mo-ses, God's cho-sen, lived long by Pha-raoh's side. ___
"Go back now to E-gypt, Is-rael's rea-dy now at last." ___

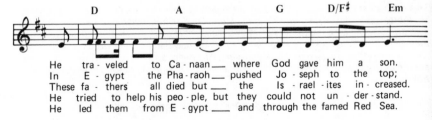

He tra-veled to Ca-naan ___ where God gave him a son.
In E-gypt the Pha-raoh ___ pushed Jo-seph to the top;
These fa-thers all died but ___ the Is-rael-ites in-creased.
He tried to help his peo-ple, but they could not un-der-stand.
He led them from E-gypt ___ and through the famed Red Sea.

Tune copyright © 1981 by Dwight Thomas. Used by permission. Words copyright © 1977 by Evangel Press, Nappanee, IN 46550; Faith and Life Press, Newton, KS 67114; Mennonite Publishing House, Scottdale, PA 15683.

Through I - saac, the pro - mised, the sto - ry's just be - gun. _____
He warned them of fam - ine and tall - ied ev - 'ry crop. _____
New ru - lers ruled E - gypt, so good times soon de - creased. ___
He fled in - to Mi - dian, a stran - ger in that land. _____
Through hard - ship and trou - ble God helped them to be free. _____

Grades 5/6 Year I Quarter 1

The King of Glory **105**

Linea R. Geiser

Traditional Israeli folk song

Chorus

Prophet: Who is the king of Glo - ry? Nev - er for - get.

Yah - weh the Lord Al - might - y is reign - ing yet.

Verses

People: 1 We want a hu - man king like all of the na - tions
2 Saul is the king of Is - rael. Let's bow be - fore him,
3 Saul dis - o - beyed the Lord What shall we do? _____
4 Here comes a son of Jes - se, Da - vid by name. _____
5 Da - vid is old and fee - ble. Who is our new king?
Slower: 6 Ju - dah and Is - ra - el a - gainst each oth - er.

Sam - uel a - noint a king. We've run out of pa - tience.
Com - ing to rule us now. We will o - bey him!
He will be king no more. God's warn - ing came true! _____
He'll rule in place of Saul. ___ Let's shout his fame: _____
Sol - o - mon or A - don - i - jah? For whom shall we sing?
Twelve tribes are not u - nit - ed with one a - noth - er.

106 Noah's Song

Connie Wiebe Isaac

Dwight Thomas

Verses

1 No - ah built an ark of wood, Built it like God said he should.
2 Friends said, "What a cra - zy boat!" Neigh-bors laughed, "It'll nev - er float."
3 Beasts and birds came two by two, Walked or jumped or crawled or flew.
4 Folks cried, "Get your boats and row!" No - ah said, "Ain't no place to go."
5 But the door was bolt - ed tight, God had shut it by his might.

"Make that ark four hun - dred feet, Seal the wood so it won't leak."
God said, "Bring the an - i - mals in, Time for the judge-ment to be - gin!"
Rain - drops fell down from the sky, Fell right in the neigh-bor's eye.
"No - ah, o - pen up your door, We won't laugh at you no more!"
Rain was cold and the wa-ter was deep, No - ah's fam - 'ly safe did keep.

Chorus

See the rain - bow af - ter the rain. God won't send the flood a - gain!

Tune copyright © 1980 by Dwight Thomas. Used by permission. Text copyright © 1977 by Evangel Press, Nappanee, IN 46550; Faith and Life Press, Newton, KS 67114; Mennonite Publishing House, Scottdale, PA 15683.

107 You'll Have a Son

Marian Hochstetler

Dwight Thomas

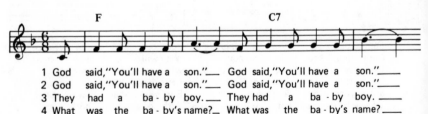

1 God said, "You'll have a son."___ God said, "You'll have a son."___
2 God said, "You'll have a son."___ God said, "You'll have a son."___
3 They had a ba - by boy. ___ They had a ba - by boy. ___
4 What was the ba - by's name?___ What was the ba - by's name?___

God said, "You'll have a son," and A - bra - ham _____ laughed.
God said, "You'll have a son," and Sar - ah _____ laughed.
They had a ba - by boy, and Sar - ah laughed for joy.
What was the ba - by's name? His name _____ was _____ "Laughed."

Laughed, laughed, laughed. A - bra - ham _____ laughed. _____
Laughed, laughed, laughed. Sar - ah _____ laughed. _____
Laughed, laughed, laughed. Sar - ah laughed for joy. _____
Laughed, laughed, laughed. His name _____ was _____ "Laughed." _____

Laughed, laughed, laughed. A - bra - ham _____ laughed.
Laughed, laughed, laughed. Sar - ah _____ laughed.
Laughed, laughed, laughed. Sar - ah laughed for joy.
Laughed, laughed, laughed. His name _____ was _____ "Laughed."

Grades 5/6 Year I Quarter 2

Dry Bones

108

Traditional

Spiritual

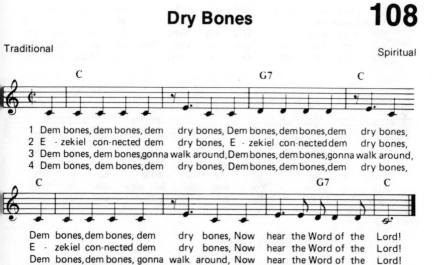

1 Dem bones, dem bones, dem dry bones, Dem bones, dem bones, dem dry bones,
2 E - zekiel con-nected dem dry bones, E - zekiel con-nected dem dry bones,
3 Dem bones, dem bones, gonna walk around, Dem bones, dem bones, gonna walk around,
4 Dem bones, dem bones, dem dry bones, Dem bones, dem bones, dem dry bones,

Dem bones, dem bones, dem dry bones, Now hear the Word of the Lord!
E - zekiel con-nected dem dry bones, Now hear the Word of the Lord!
Dem bones, dem bones, gonna walk around, Now hear the Word of the Lord!
Dem bones, dem bones, dem dry bones, Now hear the Word of the Lord!

109   The Song of Adam

Phyllis Martens

Darrel Hostetler

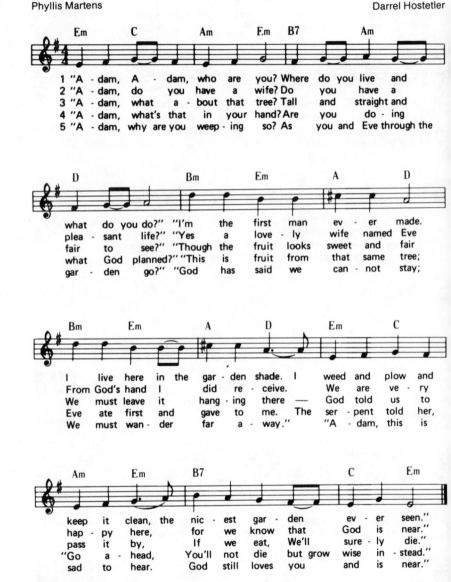

Alternative tune: "Twinkle, Twinkle, Little Star."

Go Down, Moses

110

Spiritual

Verses

1 When Is - rael was in E - gypt's land, Let my peo - ple go!
2 "Thus saith the Lord,"bold Mos - es said, "Let my peo - ple go!

Op - pressed so hard they could not stand, Let my peo - ple go!
If not, I'll smite your first - born dead, Let my peo - ple go!"

Chorus

Go down, Mo - ses, 'way down in E - gypt's land ____

Tell __ ol' Phar - aoh, Let my peo - ple go.

3 No more shall they in bondage toil,
Let them come out with Egypt's
spoil.
4 When Israel out of Egypt came,
And left the proud oppressive land.
5 Oh, 'twas a dark and dismal night,
When Moses led the Israelites.
6 'Twas good ol' Moses and Aaron,
too,
"Twas they that led the armies
through."
7 The Lord told Moses what to do,
To lead the children of Israel
through.
8 O come along, Moses, you'll not get
lost,
Stretch out your rod and come
across.
9 As Israel stood by the water side,
At the command of God it did divide.
10 When they had reached the other
shore,
They sang the song of triumph o'er.

11 Pharaoh said he would go across,
But Pharaoh and his host were lost.
†12 Oh, Moses, the cloud shall clear the
way,
A fire by night, a shade by day.
†13 You'll not get lost in the wilderness,
With a lighted candle in your breast.
†14 Jordan shall stand up like a wall,
And the walls of Jericho shall fall.
*†15 Your foes shall not before you stand,
And you'll possess fair Canaan's
land.
†16 'Twas just about in harvesttime,
When Joshua led his host divine.
*17 Oh, let us all from bondage flee,
And let us all in Christ be free.
18 We need not always weep and
moan,
And wear these slavery chains
forlorn.

*Verses sung on 3/4 Year II Quarter 1 demonstration tape.
†Verses sung on 3/4 Year II Quarter 2 demonstration tape.

111   Fear Not! Rejoice and Be Glad

Adapted from Joel 2,3,4

Priscilla Wright

har - vest is ripe, the Lord___ has giv - en us rain. ___
foun - tain of life, my chil - dren will know they are mine. ___
geth - er a - gain, my Spir - it will show them the way. ___
Fa - ther a - bove, my bo - dy will set man - kind free. ___

Gather Together

112

(A Round)

Esther Groves

♩ = 108

I Bm (Am)✱ A (G) G (F) F♯ (E) Bm(Am)

Hebrews: Gath - er to-geth-er to re - mem - ber God our Fa - ther's might - y deeds.
Christians: Gath - er to-geth-er to re - mem - ber your el-der Broth-er, Je - sus Christ;

II Bm (Am) A (G) G (F) F♯ (E) Bm(Am)

God saved us from sla - v'ry and gave us his ho - ly law;
Liv - ing, teach - ing, heal - ing and dy - ing to show us love,

III Bm (Am) A (G) G (F) F♯ (E) Bm(Am)

So that we be - come his peo - ple, liv - ing God's way as our praise.
So we know what love is like, and show love ev - 'ry - where on earth.

*To use chords in ( ), capo 2nd fret on the guitar.

113 By the Babylonian Rivers

E. J. Bash
Based on Psalm 137:1-4

Latvian melody

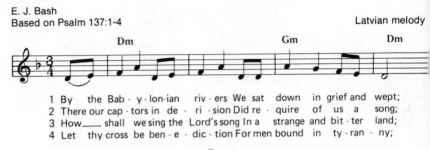

1 By the Bab - y - lon-ian riv - ers We sat down in grief and wept;
2 There our cap - tors in de - ri - sion Did re - quire of us a song;
3 How___ shall we sing the Lord's song In a strange and bit - ter land;
4 Let thy cross be ben - e - dic - tion For men bound in ty - ran - ny;

Hanged our harps up - on a wil - low, Mourned for Zi - on when we slept.
So we sat with star-ing vi - sion, And the days were hard and long.
Can our voi - ces veil the sor - row? Lord God, hold thy ho - ly band.
By the pow'r of res - ur - rec-tion Loose them from cap - ti - vi - ty.

114 God Gave a Promise

Marian Hostetler

Folk tune

1 God gave a prom - ise, God gave a prom - ise,
2 God kept his prom - ise, God kept his prom - ise,
3 God gave a prom - ise, God gave a prom - ise,
4 God kept his prom - ise, God kept his prom - ise,
5 God gave a prom - ise, God gave a prom - ise,
6 God kept his prom - ise, God kept his prom - ise,

God gave a prom - ise, "You soon will have a son."
God kept his prom - ise when I - saac was born.
God gave a prom - ise, "This land it will be yours."
God kept his prom - ise, ___ af - ter ma - ny years.
God gave a prom - ise, ___ "I will make you great."
God kept his prom - ise. He's keep - ing it to - day.

Here We Go A-Caroling

115

(A Song for All the Seasons)

Words and music by
Richard Avery and Donald Marsh

1 Here we go a - car - ol - ing, a - car - ol - ing, a - car - ol - ing,
2 At Je - sus' birth a - won - der - ing, a - won - der - ing, a - won - der - ing,
3 At his death a - sor - row - ing, a - sor - row - ing, a - sor - row - ing,
4 So we go a - car - ol - ing, a - car - ol - ing, a - car - ol - ing,

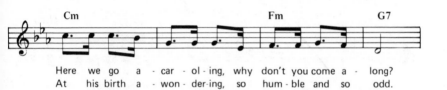

Here we go a - car - ol - ing, why don't you come a - long?
At   his birth a - won - der - ing, so hum - ble and so odd.
At   his death a - sor - row - ing, to see the end of love.
So   we go a - car - ol - ing, as he would have us do;

From the gos - pel bor - row - ing, a - bor - row - ing, a - bor - row - ing,
To   his words a - lis - ten - ing, a - lis - ten - ing, a - lis - ten - ing,
At   his ris - ing mar - vel - ing, a - mar - vel - ing, a - mar - vel - ing,
With his gos - pel trav - el - ing, a - trav - el - ing, a - trav - el - ing

From the gos - pel bor - row - ing and turn - ing it to song.
To   his words a - lis - ten - ing a - bout the love of God.
At   his ris - ing mar - vel - ing the won - ders from a - bove.
With his gos - pel trav - el - ing to ev - 'ry one like you.

116   **What Child Is This?**

William Chatterton Dix, c. 1865   Traditional English melody

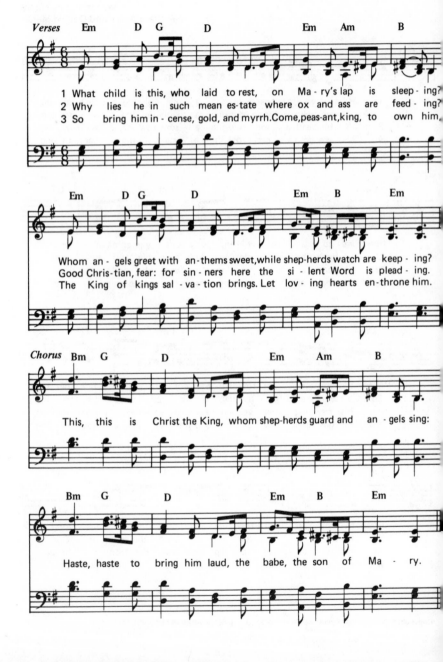

1 What child is this, who laid to rest, on Ma - ry's lap is sleep - ing?
2 Why lies he in such mean es - tate where ox and ass are feed - ing?
3 So bring him in - cense, gold, and myrrh. Come, peas - ant, king, to own him,

Whom an - gels greet with an - thems sweet, while shep-herds watch are keep - ing?
Good Chris - tian, fear: for sin - ners here the si - lent Word is plead - ing.
The King of kings sal - va - tion brings. Let lov - ing hearts en - throne him.

Chorus

This, this is Christ the King, whom shep-herds guard and an - gels sing:

Haste, haste to bring him laud, the babe, the son of Ma - ry.

This Is Christmas Morn

117

T.C.E.

Theresa C. Eshbach

Verse lines (beneath the music):

1 Shep-herds a-lone in the fields, ___ On-ly their lambs ___ were near. ___ A star and a voice broke the qui-et night; They shook in their shoes ___ with fear. ___ Don't be a-fraid, my friends, ___ For this is Christ-mas morn! ___ This ver-y night in Da-vid's town Your Sav-ior, Christ, was born. ___

2 The shep-herds just stood in a-maze-ment; Dumb-found-ed they gazed at the sky; ___ When just at that mo-ment a great an-gel choir Sang prais-es to God ___ on high. ___ Peace on the earth, my friends, ___ For this is Christ-mas morn! ___

3 * Wise men of great fame and for-tune Saw the new star bold-ly shine. ___ They knew it was his, so they hur-ried-ly came, With gifts so ex-qui-site-ly fine. ___ Joy comes to you, my friends, ___ For this is Christ-mas morn! ___

4 To-night we re-mem-ber his com-ing. What is your off-'ring to him? ___ A life that will shine just as bright as that star, Or one that's grown dark ___ and dim? ___ Love comes to you, my friends, ___ Yes, this is Christ-mas morn! ___

*"Three men" on the demonstration tape. Verse 4 is not sung on the demonstration tape.

118

Jesus

Music and words
by A. N. Rupp

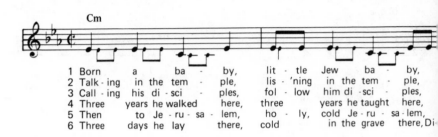

Cm

```
1 Born          a      ba  -  by,      lit - tle   Jew   ba  -  by,
2 Talk - ing    in the tem -     ple,  lis - 'ning in the tem -  ple,
3 Call - ing    his di - sci -   ples,  fol - low  him di - sci - ples,
4 Three         years he walked  here,  three      years he taught here,
5 Then          to Je - ru - sa - lem,  ho -  ly,   cold Je - ru - sa - lem,
6 Three         days he lay      there, cold       in the grave   there, Di-
```

```
Je - sus,    the   man - ger    child.
Je - sus,    the   man - boy     tall.
Je - sus,    in    Ga - li -      lee.
Je - sus,    the   heal - ing    power.
Je - sus,    the   Son   of       God.           Be -
sci - ples         sad - ly    mourned.
```

Cm   **Fm**

```
Beth - le - hem to  E - gypt,       dark,  fear - ful   E - gypt, For
Par - ents could-n't find   him,    thought he was be - hind  them, But
Phar - i - sees de-spised    him,    scribes  did-n't  like    him, And
Down   through Pe - re - a,  Sa - mar - i - a, Ju - de - a,   He
tray - al   in the gar - den,        man - y hearts were hard-ened, They
Third       day God raised  him,     earth and heav - en praise him.
```

Cm   **Gm**   **Cm**

```
Her - od had grown an-gry and  wild. Oh, _ Beth-le-hem to E - gypt,
Je - sus was-n't there       at all.  Oh, _ par-ents could-n't find him,
planned  how to make  him   die,   Oh, _ Phar-i-sees de-spised him, Sa
moved in-to his last  dark  hour.  Oh, _ down  through Pe-re-a,
nailed his bod-y to   the   wood.  Oh, be-tray-al  in the gar-den,
Death is dead and Christ is our Lord, Oh, _ third  day God raised him,
```

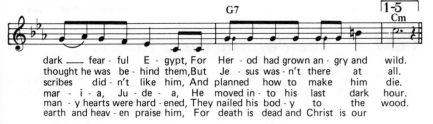

dark ___ fear - ful E - gypt, For Her - od had grown an - gry and wild.
thought he was be - hind them, But Je - sus was - n't there at all.
scribes did - n't like him, And planned how to make him die.
mar - i - a, Ju - de - a, He moved in - to his last dark hour.
man - y hearts were hard - ened, They nailed his bod - y to the wood.
earth and heav - en praise him, For death is dead and Christ is our

Lord, Al - le - lu - ia! Death is dead and Christ is our Lord!

Grades 1/2 Year II Quarter 3

Row, Row, Row Your Boat **119**

(A Round)

Rosella Weins Regier   Traditional

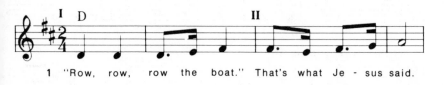

1 "Row, row, row the boat." That's what Je - sus said.

"Row the boat to the oth - er side while I take a nap."

2 Whoooo, whoooo, went the wind.
  Rain came splashing down.
  "Jesus, won't you please wake up?
  *We're scared; we're sinking fast."

3 Jesus stood and looked around.
  "Peace be still," he said.
  "Don't be frightened. I am here."
  And so they rowed again.

*This is the line as sung on the demonstration tape.
The song "Spinning, Twirling," Grades 1/2 Year II Quarter 4, may also be sung to this tune.

120   The Way, The Truth, The Life

A. G. K.
Adapted from John 14:6

Anita Grund Koch

I Am the Door

121

John 10:9, 14, 27-30

Sheilagh Nowacki

Chorus

I am the Door. I am the Shep-herd. I know my sheep and am known of mine.

I am the Door.   I am the Shep-herd. My sheep hear my voice and they fol-low me.

And I give to them ___ e - ter-nal life ___ and they shall nev-er__ per - ish.

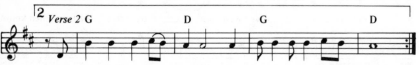

And they shall nev-er__ per - ish, nor ev - er be ta - ken from me.

They shall   nev-er be ta - ken from me, for my Fa-ther who gave them is

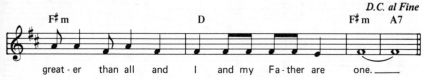

great - er   than   all   and   I   and my Fa-ther are   one. ___

122   A New Commandment

John 13:34-35

Composer unknown
Arr. by Dwight Thomas

ci - ples, if you have love one for a - noth - er. _____

Grades 7/8 Year II Quarter 3

Well, It's a New Day **123**

Words and music by J. H. Miffleton

Chorus

Well, it's a new_____ day, Think new thoughts, for there's a

new _____ way, Change your hearts, there's a new law in the land. _____

Verses

1 A man can_____ kill with a knife of _____ steel, with a
2 An eye for an eye, and a tooth for a tooth, _____
3 _____ You shall _____ love the _____ Lord your_____ God, and your

gun, a _____ bomb or a lance.
That was the law of the land. } 1-3 But there's a new law
neigh - bor _____ as your - selves.

there's a New_____ Law { 1 A man can_____ kill with a glance.
2 _____ Love makes a great - er de - mand.
3 _____ Love your_____ en - e - my as well.

The chorus and the last phrase of the chorus ("there's a new law in the land") are repeated the last time through on the demonstration tape.

124   Teach Me Kingdom Ways

N. M.

Nancy Miner, 1975

Refrain

Refrain

Bm — Em — Bm

Teach me king - dom ways so that I may walk with thee,

F#

Teach me king - dom ways so that I may walk with thee,

Bm — Em — Bm

Teach me king - dom ways so that I may walk with thee,

Em — Bm

till I stand be - fore your throne, pre - cious Lord, glo - ry,

F# — Bm — *Fine*

glo - ry, till I stand be - fore your throne, pre - cious Lord. ____

Verses

A — D — Bm

1 In a world of chains, teach me how to be free,
2 In a world of sin, teach me how to be pure,

Em — Bm — F#m — Bm

In a world of masks, teach me how to be me.
In a world of doubts, teach me how to be sure.

A — D — Bm

Let me walk in peace in a world where there is none.
Let me walk in pow'r in a world ____ that is weak.

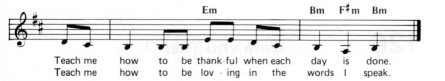

Teach me how to be thank-ful when each day is done.
Teach me how to be lov - ing in the words I speak.

Grades 5/6 Year I Quarter 3

Come and See

(Children's Song)

125

M. H. H.

Marilyn Houser Hamm

1 "Come and see, come and see, I am the way and the truth," said he.
2 Ky - ri - e, Ky - ri - e, Ky - ri - e e - le - i - son,

"Fol - low me, fol - low me, come as a child, O come and see."
Chris - te, Chris - te, Chris - te, e - le - i - son.

Descant

Chris - te, Chris - te, A - do - ra - mus te,

Melody

3 Ky - ri - e, Ky - ri - e, Ky - ri - e e - le - i - son,

Al - le - lu - ia, Ky - ri - e e - le - i - son.

Chris - te, Chris - te, Chris - te, e - le - i - son.

126

Were You There?

Traditional

Were you there when they cru - ci - fied my Lord?

Were you there when they cru - ci - fied my Lord? O!

Some-times it caus - es me to trem - ble, trem - ble, trem - ble.

Were you there when they cru - ci - fied my Lord?

2 they nailed him to the tree . . .

3 they laid him in the tomb . . .

4 he rose up from the grave . . .

Lament

127

Music and words by A. N. Rupp

♩. = 44

1 You walked through the crowds with your gen-tle-ness,_ Your cour - age and
2 You talked with the ones who were fol - low - ing,_ The par - a - ble
3 You ate with your friends in the eve - ning,_ You prayed as your
4 You stood be - fore high priests and rul - ers,_ You bent as the
5 The world now seems drear - y and emp - ty,_ The hopes you ful -

strength touched us too; You held a small child, healed the lame and the blind,
les - sons were new; We ea - ger - ly heard your com - pas - sion-filled words,
time near - er drew; "Not my will be done," cried God's on - ly Son,
death hun - ger grew; A voice, cold and grim, cried, "Cru - ci - fy him!"
filled weren't true; Your death on the cross has been ev - 'ry - one's loss,

1-4 And now they have done this to you. _ I am a - lone with my sor-row. _
5 Oh, why have they done this to you? _

I am a-lone with my pain. _ Lone-li-ness holds me like a child new-ly born, I

(after final chorus)

won't see my Je - sus a - gain._ A - gain _ I won't see my Je-sus a - gain. _

128 Christ, the Lord, Is Risen Today

Charles Wesley, 1739   *Lyra Davidica*, 1708

1 Christ the Lord is risen to-day, __
2 Lives a-gain our glo-rious King: __
3 Love's re-deem-ing work is done, __
4 Soar we now where Christ has led, __

Al - le - lu - ia!

Sons of men and an - gels say: __
Where, O death, is now your sting? __
Fought the fight, the bat - tle won; __
Fol-lowing our ex - al - ted head; __

Al - le - lu - ia!

Raise your joys and tri - umphs high,
Dy - ing once, he all doth save:
Death in vain for - bids him rise;
Made like him, like him we rise;

Al - le - lu - ia!

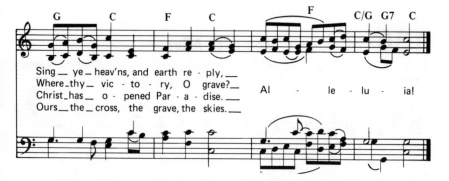

Sing — ye — heav'ns, and earth re - ply, —
Where — thy — vic - to - ry, O grave? —
Christ — has — o - pened Par - a - dise. —
Ours — the — cross, the grave, the skies. —

Al - le - lu - ia!

The D Major version found on the demonstration tape may be found in The Mennonite Hymnal, #179. A lower version is printed above in a slightly different four-part arrangement. The key of C Major should be more comfortable for young voices.

Grades 5/6 Year I Quarter 3

There Is a Green Hill Far Away   **129**

Cecil Frances Alexander, 1848

John Henry Gower, 1890

1 There is a green hill far a - way, out - side a cit - y wall,
2 We may not know, we can - not tell, what pains he had to bear;
3 He died that we might be for - giv'n, he died to make us good,
4 There was no oth - er good e - nough to pay the price of sin;
5 O dear - ly, dear - ly has he loved, and we must love him too,

Where the dear Lord was cru - ci - fied, who died to save us all.
But we be - lieve it was for us he hung and suf - fered there.
That we might go at last to heav'n, saved by his pre - cious blood.
He on - ly could un - lock the gate of heav'n, and let us in.
And trust in his re - deem - ing blood, and try his works to do.

130   **Jesus Is Alive**

C. R.

Christine Roebuck

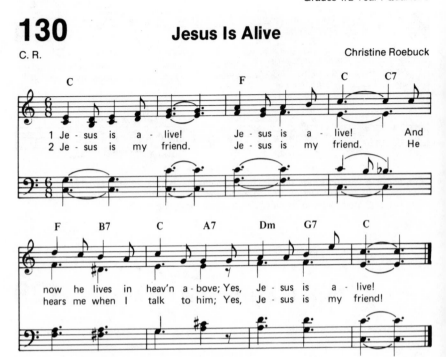

1 Je - sus is a - live!   Je - sus is a - live!   And now he lives in heav'n a - bove; Yes, Je - sus is a - live!

2 Je - sus is my friend.   Je - sus is my friend.   He hears me when I talk to him; Yes, Je - sus is my friend!

131   **Every Morning Is Easter Morning**

Words and music by
Richard Avery and Donald Marsh

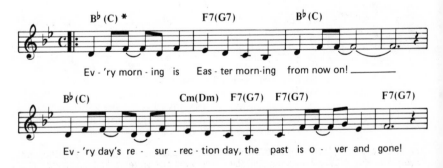

Ev - 'ry morn - ing is Eas - ter morn-ing from now on! _____

Ev - 'ry day's re - sur - rec - tion day, the past is o - ver and gone!

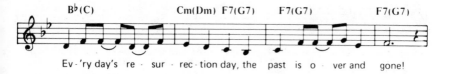

*Alternate key of C Major

Try Calypso rhythm, fast but not too fast. It should bounce joyously along. On the three final "Every morning is Easter morning" phrases, sing each one softer than the previous one. Then shout out confidently the last three words.

132　The Lord Is Risen Indeed

Thomas Kelly, 1802　　　　　　　　　　　　Arranged from Franz Joseph Haydn, 1798

1 "The Lord is ris'n in - deed," And are the tid - ings true?
2 "The Lord is ris'n in - deed," Then jus - tice asks no more;
3 "The Lord is ris'n in - deed," Then in his work per - formed;
4 "The Lord is ris'n in - deed," At - tend - ing an - gels hear;
5 Then take your gold - en lyres, And strike each cheer - ful chord

Yes, they be - held the Sav - ior bleed, and saw him
Mer - cy and truth are now a - greed, who stood op -
The cap - tive sure - ty now is freed, and death, our
Up to the courts of heav'n with speed, the joy - ful
Join all the bright ce - les - tial choirs, to sing our

liv - ing too, and saw him liv - ing too.
posed be - fore, who stood op - posed be - fore.
foe, dis - armed, and death, our foe, dis - armed.
tid - ings bear, the joy - ful tid - ings bear.
ris - en Lord, to sing our ris - en Lord.

Now May the God of Strength **133**

Adapted from Hebrews 13:20-21

German folk song
Arr. by Betty Ann Ramseth

This song may be sung as a round, or (as on the demonstration tape) sung all the way through in unison followed by the three parts in harmony. For additional verses, the words peace, joy, love, etc., may be substituted for strength.

134

Shalom Chaverim

Tr. Augustus D. Zanzig

Israeli round

Sha - lom cha - ve-rim! Sha - lom cha-ve-rim! Sha - lom, Sha - lom!
Fare - well, good friends, Fare - well, good friends, Fare - well, Fare - well!

Le - hit - ra - ot, le - hit - ra - ot, Sha - lom, Sha - lom!
Till we meet a - gain, till we meet a - gain, Fare - well, Fare - well!

Alphabetical Index

This alphabetical listing of songs include titles found throughout the entire Foundation Series. Songs printed in this book, from Grades 1-8, are indicated by bold type followed by a page number. By turning to any particular song, you will find further information about the Grades, Year, and Quarter in which the song is found. Songs not found in this book are listed in this index along with their location in the curriculum.

Symbols used are:

cs = cassette only

K = Kindergarten

LS = *Let's Sing* preschool songbook

N = Nursery

Q = Quarter

SWM = *Sing With Me* preschool songbook

wo = words only

Y = Year

Yth = Youth

* = Keyboard accompaniment printed

Curriculum Index

(Grades 1-8, only songs printed in this book)

After you determine what Year and Quarter is currently in use in your Sunday school, you may look here to see what the children are singing at their grade level. It is good to reinforce these songs in assemblies, worship services, club groups, or at home. You will notice that some songs are printed in this book which appear in the curriculum on the demonstration tape only. Children who are good listeners will enjoy singing these songs. A handful of other songs are found in print and on tapes which do not appear in this book.

*denotes printed keyboard accompaniment

denotes printed keyboard accompaniment

Topical Index

(Grades 1-8, only songs printed in this book)

*denotes printed keyboard accompaniment

*denotes printed keyboard accompaniment

Music on Demonstration Cassette Tapes

(Grades 1-8)